In this research, I used materials from the World Wide Web as well as books and journal articles. All who wish to know more about the subject this book presents may find what they seek on the World Wide Web. Research over the past decades has placed my thinking in the middle of this phenomenon and as a professional teacher I have developed my own perspective. I firmly believe that true originality lies in a new insight to past information, and ingenuity in the interpretation of old data.

A wise King once said, "...there is no new thing under the sun," Consequently, in an effort to digest the mass of available material, I may have quoted some authors inadvertently.

Land of Rising Ghosts & Goblins

The supernatural world in Japanese Myths, Folklores, Anime & Pop-Culture

Isao Ebihara

Post Gutenberg™

AN IMPRINT OF
GLOBALEDADVANCEPRESS

Land of Rising Ghosts & Goblins

The supernatural world in Japanese Myths, Folklores, Anime & Pop-Culture

Copyright © 2012 by Isao Ebihara

Library of Congress Control Number: 2012950130
Land of Rising Ghosts and Goblins
ISBN 978-1-935434-12-2

Subject Codes and Description: 1. REL017000 Religion: Comparative Religion
2. HIS021000 History: Asia - Japan 3. LIT008030 Literary Criticism: Asian -
Japanese

Printed in Australia, Brazil, France, Germany, Italy, Spain, UK, and USA.

Cover Design by Gayle Etcheverry

The Press does not have ownership of the contents of a book; this is
the author's work and the author owns the copyright. All theory, concepts,
constructs, and perspectives are those of the author and not necessarily the
Press. They are presented for open and free discussion of the issues involved. All
comments and feedback should be directed to the Email: [*comments4author@
aol.com*] and the comments will be forwarded to the author for response.

Published by

Post-Gutenberg Books™

An Imprint of

GlobalEdAdvance Press

www.gea-books.com

Dedication

To Hiroshi & Noriko Ebihara

& Nyanta their late feline son

(1996 - 2009)

Table of Contents

Foreword

My previous two books introduced Japanese religious tradition and spiritual culture to those from outside the Japanese culture.

For the past century, Japan has been a centre of attention from the global community because of her rapid industrialization and modernization. A large number of ambitious scholars called "Japanologists" have spent tremendous amounts of time and energy to study this mysterious land. However, certain aspects of the nation's culture remain an enigma and are inscrutable for almost all outsiders and even by some insiders of the land. Particularly, the religious and spiritual aspects of the culture have failed to be correctly interpreted and therefore, remain a mystery. I do not claim that my books are the sole key to solve mysteries in the Far East. However, I hope that my work might give the students of East Asia new insight into Japanese culture and spirituality.

In the first book, I introduced and discussed extensively religious and spiritual culture in several anime and manga authors. In the second book, I introduced a sect of Shinto religion that was linked closely with Japanese nationalist politics and imperialist military expenditure before the Second World War. I examined the historical formation of their spirituality and potential danger of reviving it in the future.

In this third book, I am going to introduce the same subject matter. This book discusses the world of ghosts, spirits, supernatural phenomena and incidents in Japanese mythology, folklore and legends from antiquity to novels, anime and manga from modernity and post-modernity. How did Japanese from antiquity to the modern day draw pictures of the spiritual and supernatural world? What kind of afterlife did they envision? Do they still believe in the afterlife and the supernatural in the 21st century? Are there any similarities and differences from the afterlife and spiritual world that westerners describe?

These are the questions I seek to answer and trust that this book will provide at least one key to understanding this intricate and sometimes obscure subject.

Dr. Stephen Hawking (b.1942)[1], a well respected physicist from Britain, made a series of stunning statements in his book *The Grand Design* (2010)[2]. He states there is no designer of the universe. He maintains that the universe and its living and non-living components came into existence by chance. In May, 2011, he made another statement that there is no heaven, hell or life after death. He made an analogy to compare the dead with a broken computer, and concluded neither of them have any afterlife after they cease to operate. According to him, a belief that heaven or an afterlife awaits us is a "fairy story" for people afraid of death. He asserted that we see nothing beyond the moment when the brain flickers for the final time.

Those who lived in antiquity, however, were afraid of the misfortunes that they might encounter after the end of their earthly life far more than the death itself. Therefore, they might state that Hawking's belief is a "fairy story" because they were

---

1   Wikipedia: Stephen Hawking. Online at http://en.wikipedia.org/wiki/Stephen_Hawking

2   Stephen Hawking. The Grand Design. (NY: USA: Random House Publishing Group, 2011)

people afraid of the eternal torments in Hades or the next life coming back to this world as animals or lower and less intelligent life forms.

Those who live in the modern world tend to incline to Hawking's belief as the most rational acceptable theory. But those who lived in the ancient world would regard this theory as absurd, irrational and strange, except perhaps a handful of minorities like Sadducees in Israel. Sadducees in Israel during the New Testament era denied life after the tomb, yet firmly believed in the existence of a one and only God and supernatural activities by him and his angels. On the other hand, Buddhism and Shinto beliefs are atheistic in the sense that they deny the existence of a creator or a monotheistice view of a God of this universe. However, they firmly believed in the supernatural domain of the universe.

Hawking denies God, the supernatural, and the afterlife. But it was extremely rare or nearly impossible in the ancient world to deny all three of these simultaneously. The denial of God, the supernatural, and afterlife, or all of three, is clearly a product of modernism, the philosophy of Enlightenment in the 18th century and Marxism in the 19th and 20th century, which are already obsolete. Philosophers in that modern era tried to establish world views without God, in which humans were masters and de facto leaders of this world. Decisions that people made were seen as absolute authority because they replaced God as the ruler of the universe. Friedrich Nietzsche (1844–1900)[3] stated, "God is dead", and Karl Marx (1818–1883)[4] advocated the concepts of dialectical materialism and

---

3   Wikipedia: Friedrich Nietzsche. Online at http://en.wikipedia.org/wiki/Friedrich_Nietzsche
4   Wikipedia: Karl Marx. Online at http://en.wikipedia.org/wiki/Karl_Marx

regarded religion as opium. In my observation, Hawking simply follows the obsolete philosophy of modernism more than science. His belief is not as inventive as Nietzsche and Marx, who created new theories from a previous era. As a scientist, however, he must be well aware of the fact that science will never prove his assumption that there is no life after the grave.

It is within this context of the ancient beliefs, in contrast to the beliefs of Hawking, and other modernists and post modernists, that the discussion of Japanese spirituality will take place.

Introduction

Historical Formation of Japanese Concept of
Afterlife & Spiritual World

The uniqueness of the Japanese afterlife concept lies in the fact that the inhabitants of the archipelago adopted both Buddhism coming from India through China and Shinto, the archaic Japanese belief system. In the Shinto tradition, there are two predominant thoughts about the afterlife.

The first concept is that some individuals with remarkable achievements are enhanced into Kami (神) or Shinto deity at the end of this earthly life. This part of the belief system is what makes Shinto Kami distinct from Greek and Roman deities or most other polytheistic belief systems in the world. The deities in the Greco-Roman mythologies had no past as humans, since they were born as gods. Kojiki, the oldest Japanese literary work, which includes the myth of the Imperial family and origin of the nation, describes how heroes or illustrious warriors in the Shinto myth and some other brave people became Kami after death.

The second concept is that the souls of the dead are expected to go to a dark afterlife, the Land of Yomi. According to Kojiki, this is like a Hades where all are destined to go. This is an apparent contradiction because all are going regardless of their conduct during their lifetime. This idea of Yomi or Hades that both good and bad people were destined to go was obviously not a comfort for most Japanese. After the introduction of Buddhism and literacy from China around the

Seventh Century, Japan became a society with a dual faith of Shinto and Buddhism. Following that, people usually conducted funerals in Buddhist temples because they didn't want to go to the Land of Yomi.

However, some theorists maintain that the primitive Shinto supported an afterlife concept similar to reincarnation. According to them, the term "Kami" in the most archaic Proto-Shinto usually indicated dead people, or those who were gone to "Yomi" and are not yet come back to the world of the living.

Buddhism also has two different and apparently conflicting concepts about the afterlife. One is "transmigration of souls," the most well known afterlife concept of Buddhism. In this, there is neither heaven nor hell in which the dead are destined to go. They simply have a rebirth after death either as a human or animal, depending on their conduct during their lifetime. If a subject has virtuous and honorable conduct throughout their entire life, he or she will be reincarnated into a family with more wealth and higher prestige. In the ideal scenario, this person might even be an emperor or empress. On the other hand, if a person has poor behavior and a dishonorable lifestyle, he or she will be born into the next life in poverty and a lower socioeconomic status. In the worst scenario, this person may be an animal and consumed as food by some other humans or animals.

The second well known afterlife concept of Buddhism is a migration to the [5]Pure Land or the celestial realm which belongs to Buddha or Bodhisattva. Pure Land is a Buddhist heaven in which only those with good conduct and character

---

5   Wikipedia: Pure Land. Online at http://en.wikipedia.org/wiki/Pure_land

are allowed to enter. The [6]Mahāyāna Buddhists who believe in Pure Land also believe in the hell ruled by Yama[7] or Enma Dai-Ō (閻魔大王) the ruler of Hades, the destination of those whose conduct is not honorable during their lifetime. The Mahāyāna Buddhist believes that if a person migrates into the Pure Land once, he or she stays there forever, never dies and becomes another human or animal. On the other hand, there is no unanimous view about whether people may exit from the Buddhist hell or not. Some believe that hell is a final and ultimate destiny for sinners with eternal torture and gnashing pain. If someone goes to the hell once, the process is completely irreversible and there is no way to exit from there, similar to the orthodox Christians belief. Others believe that if a subject spends a certain length of time there, this person may then leave. However, one must spend millions or billions of years of torment, and he or she must start a new life from the lowest form of existence such as an insect or a worm.

After Buddhism was introduced to Japan by Prince Shotoku (b. 524) in the Seventh Century, the Japanese developed a majestic picture of their afterlife during the Heian period (平安時代794 to 1185). Because several different Buddhist concepts about the afterlife migrated to the archipelago, the Japanese developed a fear of going to hell and coming back as animals. They were not sure of the correct consequence for the worst kind of criminal. However, they believe that the criminal deserves one of the most severe punishments after death.

Apart from either Shinto or Buddhist traditions, Japanese folklore also developed their ideas about ghosts. They are

6   Wikipedia: Mahayana. Online at http://en.wikipedia.org/wiki/Mahayana_Buddhism
7   Wikipedia: Yama. Online at http://en.wikipedia.org/wiki/Yama

seen as souls of the dead that failed to migrate to either the Pure Land or hell, and remain on earth for an indefinite period of time without reincarnation into the next life. These loosely come from the Buddhist idea, since there is a belief that a person who died with vengeful thoughts, deep regrets or unfulfilled wishes and desires may stay in this world as a ghost. Patrick Lafcadio Hearn[8] (1850–1904) who went to Japan with a commission as a newspaper correspondent in the 19th century was greatly inspired by the world of ghosts that the mediaeval Japanese described. [9]He wrote several stories about ghosts in Japan in a few different historical settings and compiled them into a volume entitled "Kwaidan: Stories and Studies of Strange Things"[10].

Yōkai (妖怪)[11] is another genre of preternatural creatures in Japanese folklore and mythology. The term Yōkai is often loosely translated into "demon" in English, but they are not always evil like demons in the West and unlike followers of Lucifer the fallen archangel. They are not a homogenous spices, but a collection of various mythological creatures. Some of them were human ghosts transformed into Yōkai by some sort of extreme emotional state such as tremendously large grief, intense jealousy, rage, wrath, pain or vengeful thoughts.

Some of them are live animals, animals' ghosts, or anthromorphised animals. They are often considered kami (神) or deities as well as Yōkai, since they occasionally bring

8   Wikipedia: Lafcadio Hearn. Online at http://en.wikipedia.org/wiki/Lafcadio_Hearn
9   Wikipedia: Kwaidan: Stories and Studies of Strange Things. Online at http://en.wikipedia.org/wiki/Kwaidan:_Stories_and_Studies_of_Strange_Things
10   Lafcadio Hearn. *Kwaidan: Stories and Studies of Strange Things.* (Tokyo, Japan: Tuttle Publishing, 1971)
11   Wikipedia: Yōkai. Online at http://en.wikipedia.org/wiki/Y%C5%8Dkai

great benefits and fortunes to humans. For instance, Inari Ōkami, (稲荷大神)[12] the fox god, is one of the principal deities of Shinto and the symbol of worldly success, as well as a well known animal, Yōkai. Inari appears to be an object of worship since the founding of a shrine at Inari Mountain in 711 AD, that consequently spread across Japan. Since Inari was a popular figure in both Shinto and Buddhist beliefs, many country houses of wealthy families host their shrines.

Since Ōkami (大神) means "big god" and wolves at the same time, it is generally canine deities or Yōkai in Japanese mythology. There are a variety of canines like foxes, wolves, tanuki or raccoon dogs and domestic dogs that are deified and sometimes anthromorphised in Japanese myths and folklores.

InuYasha, a Feudal Fairy Tale or Sengoku Otogizōshi InuYasha (戦国御伽草子犬夜叉)[13] is an anime and manga series created by Rumiko Takahashi (b. 1957). The main character is a half human and half dog Yōkai warrior who lives in the Sengoku period (戦国時代) or 15th Century to the beginning of the 17th Century. InuYasha is a typical anthropomorphic animal, Yōkai, since he has a human figure with canine ears. Yōkai and humans in Japanese legends often mate and produce mixed offspring, although these two are completely different life forms. The term yasha (夜叉) stems from from yaksha in Hindu and Buddhist mythology in India. In Indian myth, yaksha is either a harmless nature-fairy or a ghost that haunts the wilderness and attacks travelers.

Another well-known category of Yōkai in Japanese folklore is Oni (鬼)[14], a mountain-dwelling ogre with a slight

---

12   Wikipedia: Inari Ōkami. Online at http://en.wikipedia.org/wiki/Inari_Okami
13   Wikipedia: InuYasha. Online at http://en.wikipedia.org/wiki/InuYasha
14   Wikipedia: Oni (folklore). Online at http://en.wikipedia.org/wiki/Oni_(folklore)

resemblance to Shrek.[15] The character (鬼) simply means spirit or ghost of the dead in China. However, Japanese developed the image of Oni, a humanoid with sharp claws, wild hair, and two long horns growing from their heads, wearing loincloths made of tiger-skin and carrying iron clubs. The humanoid figure of Oni could be stemmed from Yaksha[16] from Buddhist mythology in India instead of China.

Some of them live on earth and some others live in hell or several different dimensions of the universe. They are usually antagonistic to humans and greatly feared by people, so that the term Oni is frequently translated as demons or devils. Those who live on earth are sometimes anthropophagus and consume human flesh as food. However, some are good, make friends with people and great contributions to society.

In the Hell that the Japanese describe, sinners are punished and tormented by these creatures forever. However, some Oni are amiable to mankind and often bring great benefits to humanity. Oni who dwell in the earthly realm periodically transform into humans and live like them, since they have the power to morph. Like many other kinds of Yōkai, Oni are able to mate with humans and produce mixed offspring.

They have both genders; however, more males are introduced into the legends and folklore. Mediaeval Japanese believed that some human ghosts who died with an extreme emotional state like jealousy or rage often transformed into Oni. For instance, Hannya (般若)[17] is a female Oni who was once a jealous and vengeful human female. However, most of

---

15   Wikipedia: Shrek. Online at http://en.wikipedia.org/wiki/Shrek
16   Wikipedia: Yaksha. Online at http://en.wikipedia.org/wiki/Yaksha
17   Wikipedia: Hannya (般若). Online at http://en.wikipedia.org/wiki/Hannya

them are separate entities from the humanity that bred them despite the fact they are humanoid species living close to mankind.

Tengu (天狗)[18] or "heavenly dogs" are another class of supernatural creatures classified as Yōkai, as well as Shinto kami found in Japanese folklore and legends. Although their name has an origin stemmed from the Chinese canine spirit, in Japan they are depicted as both humans with extraordinary big noses and avian characteristics.

Besides that, there are various animal Yōkai with configurations of felines, reptiles and avian creatures. Japan has a rich soil to produce them since Buddhists believe that animals have souls and afterlife as well as humans.

---

18   Wikipedia: Tengu. Online at http://en.wikipedia.org/wiki/Tengu

[19] Inuyasha. Takahashi, Rumiko (b. 1957) [20].

---

19   Was available May 2011: http://6kaori9.blog2.fc2.com/blog-entry-224.html
20   The picture is used under "fair dealing" (Canada) and "fair use" (USA) provisions in copyright law.

1

Spiritual World from Kojiki & Nihonshoki

Kojiki and Nihonshoki are two of the oldest pieces of Japanese literature written in the Seventh Century. They express the primitive Japanese conciousness prior to the introduction of Buddhism and other concepts from China.

In the world of [21]*Kojiki*[22] (古事記: A.D. 712) and [23]*Nihonshoki*[24] (日本書紀: A.D.720), Japan's oldest twin narratives, the afterlife concept and supernatural activities that the writers present is strictly based on the primitive Shinto prior to the introduction of Buddhism to Japan around the Seventh Century.

Afterlife in Shinto & Kami as Spirits of Dead

In Shinto, some of Kami was represented by spirits of the dead who had been humans in their lifetime. This part of the belief system distinguishes Shinto Kami from Greek and Roman deities. Although Greco-Roman deities possess some similarities to Shinto Kami, their belief system has a

---

21   Wikipedia古事記. Online at http://ja.wikipedia.org/wiki/古事記
22   Wikipedia: Kojiki. Online at http://en.wikipedia.org/wiki/Kojiki
23   Wikipedia日本書紀. Online at http://ja.wikipedia.org/wiki/%E6%97%A5%E6%9C%AC%E6%9B%B8%E7%B4%80
24   Wikipedia: Nihonshoki. Online at http://en.wikipedia.org/wiki/Nihon_Shoki

clear demarcation between human and divine realms, that is, there is no way for humans to become gods. This seems to be contradicted by *Kojiki*, the oldest Japanese literary work about the myth of the Imperial family and origin of the nation that describes how heroes in the Shinto myth become Kami after the death.

Although some dead were believed to have been deified and provide the same living services and rites as Kami, the primitive Shinto generally considered death a curse and unclean event. Regarding the Shinto view on death, [25]Ono states that Shinto regarded life as good and death as evil and a curse according to the word *kegare* (穢), which meant "abnormality" or "misfortune." The Shinto religion had developed numerous taboos and stigmas concerning the death.

But there are more than one picture about the afterlife in Shinto worldview. According to *Kojiki*, the souls of the dead were expected to go to the dark afterlife, the *Land of Yomi*. This was similar to Hades where all dead were going, regardless of the conducts during their lifetime. Since the primitive Japanese disliked the idea of afterlife in Yomi, most of these ideas or rituals centred on death were derived from Buddhism that was imported from China around the seventh-century.

Minoru Haiyama (1996)[26] maintains that the primitive Shinto supported an afterlife concept similar to reincarnation. The primitive Japanese believed that the life and death were like day and night, and the dead came back to life as the day follows the night. He puts forward to the theory that the term

25   Sokyo Ono. Shinto --- The Kami Way (Rutland, Vermont, USA & Tokyo, Japan: Charles E. Tuttle company, 1962/1969) p. 108
26   Minoru Haiyama, Yamato to Nihon [Yamato and Japan]. (Tokyo: Choseisha, 1996)

"yomi," which signifies the dark place that is the destination of the dead, has the same etymological root as "yoru" which means night[27]. It is similar to the concept of yin (陰) and yang (陽), and follows a globally prevalent idea in the ancient world to link the light with life and darkness with death. However, in Buddhism, the ethical behaviour or moral conduct during the current life determines the well being in the next life. On the other hand, the Shinto based afterlife concept has nothing to do with the morality of an individual person during his or life time. All living beings continue to rotate in the cycle of life and death and take various forms simply by chance from the eternal past to the eternal future. The concept of morality was completely foreign to the Shinto based animistic world as well as the residents of the archipelago, prior to the introduction of Buddhism and Confucianism from the continent.

On the other hand, the primitive Shinto believed in magic or shamanic spells to change the destiny of an individual or even a whole nation. The rulers or tribal chiefs of archaic Japan were magi or shaman kings and queens similar to the three Eastern Kings who visited Bethlehem when Christ was born, and practiced magics and sorceries as they governed the nation[28]. Therefore, the ancestors of the Japanese emperor were Shinto high priests, shamanic kings and queens with powers to change the fate and destiny of the whole nation according to their beliefs. Lady Himiko of prehistoric Japan was a well known shaman-queen who governed the nation with magic and spells. At the same time, historians indicate that first few emperors of Japan were monarchs with a unique

---

27   After writing system was imported from China in the Seventh Century, they spell "yomi" as 黄泉 or yellow spring and "yoru" as 夜 or night. However, it does not represent preliterate Japanese etymology of these words.
28   Matthew 2:1-26

function as high-priests who exercised various seasonal agricultural rites throughout a year and shamanic power to bring in many children, a great harvest and physical and psychological wellness to the whole nation.

In the process of divination, they employed various methods to predict the events in the future. They burned a piece of a turtle shell and interpreted the resulting cracks as well as observing stars as did the magi in the New Testament. In the process of changing the destiny of an individual or the whole nation, they offered various sacrifices, probably including live humans. Since the primitive Shinto lacked the moral concept to value each human individual, they sacrificed live humans for the well being of the entire community during their religious ceremonies.

Haiyama also maintained that the term "Kami" in the most archaic Shinto usually indicated dead people, or those who were gone to "Yomi" and had not come back to the world of the living yet. At the same time, he implies that the Proto-Japanese had a belief that both male and female sexual organs were deities because they played vital roles to bring back the dead to a new life.

After the introduction of Buddhism by [29]*Shotoku Taishi* or Prince Shotoku (574-622), Japan became a society with the dual faith of Shinto and Buddhism. These coexisted in a very unique way. People usually conducted funerals in Buddhist temples because they didn't want to go to the *Land of Yomi*. But for most other occasions like weddings, New Year's celebrations and other ceremonies such as the harvest rite,

---

29   Wikipedia: Prince Shōtoku. Online at http://en.wikipedia.org/wiki/Prince_Shotoku

they retained their Shinto faith and continued these rituals as their ancestors did from antiquity.

Beliefs & Practices of Pre-historic Proto-Shinto

It is generally believed that prehistoric Japan was a more peaceful and genteel society than China, India or the Middle East in the same age period, since there was no human sacrifice, cannibalism and castration of males. However, according to Haiyama (1996)[30], this is a completely wrong assumption. Haiyama maintains that prehistoric Japan was a land of cannibalism, genital mutilation and phallic symbol worship.

In fact, these bloody, repulsive and barbaric religious practices comparable to those found in China and the Middle East were not known to the public because they were not recorded in historical documents. In fact, activities in Japan prior to the Seventh Century were not recorded because there was no writing system at that time. However, Haiyama contends that there is enough evidence to support the view that the ancient Japanese was as bloody as the populations of other parts of the world during the same time period.

According to Haiyama, we may trace back the most archaic historical roots of the Proto-Shinto religious practices to the prehistoric era named Jomon Period (縄文時代: 14,000 BC – 300 BCE)[31]. He viewed that the term "Kami" in the Proto-Japan during the Jomon period usually signified dead people, or those who died and had not yet come back to the world of the living. The term Kami also indicates flesh or meat of

---

30   Haiyama, ibid
31   Wikipedia: Jōmon period. Online at http://en.wikipedia.org/wiki/J%C5%8Dmon_period

animals or humans sacrificed for religious rituals. He maintains that the Proto-Shinto priests and priestesses used human flesh for the magical rites and consumed the flesh to increase their shamanic power.

At the same time, Haiyama contends that both male and female genitals were also "Kami" or divine objects in the archaic Shinto because they played a vital role to transport the dead to the next life. Because these organs were sacred and spiritual objects, they were often severed and offered in a shrine during rituals of Proto-Shinto. After the rites, the priests or priestesses consumed these organs in order to increase their power to continue the sacred rites, sorcery or magic in an attempt to bring a wellness to the community. Some dedicated individuals volunteered to offer their flesh to their shamans for the well-beings of the community.

He also maintains that Kojiki and other ancient documents have several covert implications of mutilating male genitals to offer them sacred offerings to gods, although they did not contain explicit statements. He contends that jades that Shinto priests wore during the performance of rituals, though recorded as stones in recorded Japanese history, were originally made of human testicles. These organs were taken from either dead or live subjects and used for various religious rituals of Proto-Shinto. This removal of reproductive organs from either live or dead subjects was essentially different from the custom of castrating males to make eunuchs serving in the court, because the severed genitals were considered sacred objects.

Haiyama also maintains that the pre-historic Proto-Japan during Jomon Period was a matriarchic society, in which women are considered superior to men, so that many men had to offer their sexual organs or sometimes whole bodies to their wives as a special meal to increase their fertility. He contends that women had more value than men because of their ability to bear children. On the other hand, they did not need as many men as women to procreate and maintain the community. We might be able to use an analogy of a poultry farm to describe a Jomon community that practiced the cannibalism. Farmers usually keep hens until they stop laying eggs. However, they keep only one or two roosters and slaughter the rest, as soon as they reach adulthood. The males are more aggressive and start fighting each other if too many of them are kept alive. In primitive Japan during the Jomon period, men could be treated like roosters in a poultry farm, and sacrificed or butchered into meat whenever they reached maturity.

In the Yayoi period (弥生時代: 300 BC to 300 AD)[32] following the Jomon era when a different ethnic group arrived from either Korea or China and conquered the aboriginal Jomon population, males increased their value. Wars between tribes became more prevalent, and they required aggressive and strong males for battle. During this period new pottery styles appeared and residents started intensive rice agriculture in paddy fields. Men were also highly valued in paddy fields since agriculture required more intense labor.

The meat of the dead was also consumed during feasts following funeral rites in pre-historic Japan. It was a generally accepted way to pay respect to the dead in those days. It carried the idea that by doing so, the dead will some day come back to the world of the living as a person from the land of

---

32   Wikipedia: Yayoi period. Online at http://en.wikipedia.org/wiki/Yayoi_period

Yomi. If those who were still living consumed their meat, he or she might return to life as their offspring in the future. It also carried the idea that the dead might return as animals if the body was consumed by animals. So bodies of the deceased were well protected from any wild beasts until the very moment of the feast after the funeral rite was over.

However, the traditions of barbaric antiquity were conveniently thrown into the realm of oblivion when Buddhism and a writing system were imported from the continent. At the same time, Confucianism, Taoism and other new philosophies and literatures were being introduced. As a result, government officials recorded past events selectively in order to maintain the appearance of a civilized nation. The memory of human flesh consumption was excluded from their documents. Court officials during the Seventh Century annihilated any traces of the savage days from the remote past that may have contradicted with the image of a genteel and cultured nation. After the introduction of Buddhism, Japanese stopped eating even animal flesh, because a vegetarian diet was considered the most civilized way of living according to the new teaching. Thus, the island nation in the Far East successfully discarded the heritage of its savage days and made a radical transformation into a civilized state.

The government officials during the Nara Period seemed to have been successful in discarding the prehistoric memory of barbarism and made it nearly completely impossible to trace back the evidence of activities and lifestyle of people before the Seventh Century. The collective memory of the Japanese of the pre-historic savage days during the Jomon Period was seemingly sealed away forever. However, Haiyama maintains that the memory of the remote past among Japanese during the Jomon Period was still inherited in the language and discourse of Kojiki, Nihonshoki and few other of the oldest documents. He contends that one might uncover several stunning hidden facts, historical events, routine of daily religious and non-religious activities of human sacrifice, as well as their belief system. According to Haiyama, we can decode hidden implications and riddles of this literature by carefully studying the language of Kojiki and other documents.

Izanagi & Izanami

Kojiki and Nihohshoki the most archaic twin narratives in Japanese history refer to a couple of progenitors of Japanese mythology. They are deities and the first married couple named Izanagi (伊邪那岐) and Izanami (伊邪那美), born of the seven divine generations in Japanese mythology. Since archaic times, primordial forms of Shinto were strongly sexual in nature and they practiced numerous rituals to increase fertility, therefore Kojiki contains sexual symbols and innuendoes.

Although the writers of later literature intentionally excluded the memories of the barbaric past, readers may trace back the lifestyle and belief system of the Proto-Japanese during the Jomon Period. Jomon people were the worshippers of a phallus removed from the body, fertility gods and various other sexual symbols, and they also practiced cannibalism, magic or shamanic mysticism. They are viewed as crude and cruel similar to several people groups in China, India and the Middle East, as they consumed human flesh, internal organs, brains and mutilated genitals for religious ceremonies, as well as regular meals. The concept of the value and dignity of each human individual was totally foreign to the Proto-Japanese.

In Kojiki, Izanagi and Izanami met each other in the heavenly court and have aconversation with sexual connotations. Shortly after this dialogue, Izanagi and Izanami have the first intercourse after a ritual which officially makes the two husband and wife. The ritual includes building a huge pillar in the sky called Ame-no-mihashira and walking around it.

The first discourse regarding the dialogue between Izanagi and Izanami contained the motif of phallic symbol worship or idea that human genitals were sacred objects, and crucial and pivotal factors to create a new life. They had a sacro-religious ritual to create a huge pillar in the sky and walking around it before having sex, because in the Proto-Shinto, sexual intercourse was one of the religious rites. A pillar in the sky might indicate a divine phallus that symbolized procreation.

The first child named Hiruko (蛭子)[33] was born deformed and was not considered deity by his parents, so that they put him into a boat and set it out to sea. However, Hiruko returned to land and was cared for by one Ebisu Saburo. He overcome many hardships and later becomes the god Ebisu (恵比須)[34] one of *Shichifukujin* or "Seven deities of good fortune." Ebisu in appearance with a fishing rod is considered as the guardian of the health of small children, fishermen, good luck, and workingmen. Kyokuten Bakin (1767 – 1848)[35] a popular writer during Edo Period, wrote a success story of Hiruko becoming a Ebisu god, one of the most respected deities among mankind, though Hiruko was born with deformity and abandoned by his parents.

---

33   In some other stories including Nimaze no Ki by Bakin, Hiruko is their third son instead of the first son.

34   Wikipedia: Ebisu (mythology). Online at http://en.wikipedia.org/wiki/Hiruko

35   Wikipedia: 曲亭馬琴. Online at http://ja.wikipedia.org/wiki/%E6%9B%B2%E4%BA%AD%E9%A6%AC%E7%90%B4

The couple had many divine children until Izanami died giving birth to the child Kagu-Tsuchi (迦具土), which meant incarnation of fire by consuming her vagina by fire. At the death of beloved Izanami, her husband was so infuriated that he beheaded the newborn baby Kagu-Tsuchi[36] with his sword named Ame no Ohabari (天之尾羽張), and slashed the baby's body into eight pieces, which became deities representing eight volcanoes. Furthermore, since Kagu-Tsuchi was a god of flames, another eight deities, which represent fire, were born of his blood.

Izanagi, struck by grief and sorrow, made up his mind to go down to the land of Yomi or Hades to look for Izamami. He searched for his wife, but initially was unable to find her since the shadows hid her appearance. However, he finally found her after a persistent search and asked her to return to the land of the living with him. However, she refused to return to the world of the living, insisting that it was too late to do so, since she had already eaten the food of the underworld. While she was sleeping, Izanagi took the comb that bound his long hair and set it alight like a flash light. Then, he discovered that his beautiful wife had transformed into a horrendous monster because she had eaten the food of the underworld and was already decomposing. Being filled with fear and terror, Izanagi started to run, intending to return to the living and abandon his wife who had transformed into Yokai or a demon in character.

The story of Izanagi going down to the underworld to bring back Izanami has close parallels to the Greek myth of Orpheus and Eurydice. However, the two stories also have two major differences. First, Izanagi and Izanami were powerful

---

36   Wikipedia: カグツチ. Online at http://ja.wikipedia.org/wiki/%E3%82%AB%E3%82%B0%E3%83%84%E3%83%81

deities, while at the same time Orpheus[37] and Eurydice were mere mortals. Second, Izanami transformed into a horrendous monster after she consumed food in Hades. When Izanagi looks prematurely at his wife in the same way as Orpheus, she revealed her new identity as a demonic creature and pursued him in order to kill him.

After Izanami was gone, Izanagi procreated several children by himself or without a spouse. Among them, [38]*Amaterasu* (天照大神) whose name literally meant to "illuminate Heaven" was the most significant deity from which the emperor of Japan descended, according to Japanese mythology. She was born from the left eye of her father *Izanagi*, the creator god, as he was bathing in a stream, in the same way as Athena was born from Zeus's head in the Greek counterpart. She was assigned to rule the realm of the heavens while one of her brothers, *Tsuki-Yomi* (月読命), the moon god, was entrusted with the realm of night, and another brother, [39] *Susa-no-Ō* (須佐之男命), a god of storm, was made a ruler of the ocean. *Tsukuyomi* was born from the right eye, and *Susa-no-Ō* from the nose of his father. *Susa-no-Ō* was a deity with a violent temperament and had conflicts with his elder sister Amaterasu and several other siblings. He slaughtered a serpent named *Yamatano Orochi* (八岐の大蛇) with an eight-forked head and an eight-forked tail. He created a divine sword named the *Kusa-nagi no tsurugi* from one of the tails of the serpent, after he dismembered the monster into pieces. Later, Susa-no-Ō gave his sister Amaterasu the Kusa-nagi no tsurugi as a gift when they finally reconciled. Then,

37   Wikipedia: Orpheus. Online at http://en.wikipedia.org/wiki/Orpheus
38   Wikipedia: Amaterasu. Online at http://en.wikipedia.org/wiki/Amaterasu
39   Wikipedia: Susanoo. Online at http://en.wikipedia.org/wiki/Susanoo

the sword became a family treasure of the Japanese imperial family, being passed throughout generations. Eventually, the sword becomes the possession of Yamato Takeru, a legendary warrior prince of the Yamato dynasty and the most significant hero in Kojiki and Nihonshoki.

The story of Izanagi and Izanami may well represent the morality of Japanese society prior to the introduction of Buddhism and Confucianism from China. They put their first born son Hiruko into a boat and set it out to the sea because he was born deformed. The civilized world would conceive this as an extreme cruelty to an innocent child. The story that Hiruko returned to land, was cared for by a fisher, overcome many hardships and became the Ebisu god might be a story created after Japan had become a more cultured nation. Writers from more civilized centuries were more sympathetic with the child of misfortune and gave him a better place than his younger siblings who were physically mighty like Heracles, but perhaps morally or ethically "disabled." Bakin[40] praised Ebisu god and despite his unfortunate upbringing made a great success. The writer in the Edo period elaborated the legend and made his own story of the guardian of fishers.

Ebisu with a fishing rod was a guardian deity for fishers, workers and small children. It was interesting that he was the only Japanese among Shichifukujin or "Seven deities of good fortune," and all others were either Chinese or Indian. It might indicate that the story was created after the introduction of Buddhism, Confucianism, Taoism and other significant philosophies and mythologies from the continent. Among indigenous Japanese deities, Ebisu was the only one who met

---

40   Wikipedia: 曲亭馬琴. Online at http://ja.wikipedia.org/wiki/%E6%9B%B2%E4%BA%AD%E9%A6%AC%E7%90%B4

the standard to join the *Seven deities of good fortune*, and his younger brother like Susa-no-Ō, with brutish and violent characters were short of the criteria of the membership.

Next, out of an intense rage and grief after losing his beloved wife, Izanagi slashed and dismembered his baby son Kagu-Tsuchi. This is also a repulsive and outrageous behaviour for most modern readers. It was very obvious that he was not responsible for his mother's death, although his body covered with flames caused a mortal burn in her vagina. Metaphorically, Kagu-Tsuchi represents the useful, but violent and uncontrollable nature of fire, and his death has a close parallel to the destiny of Prometheus,[41] a Greek deity that was punished by the god Zeus for giving fire to mankind[42]. Fire has been a blessing and curse for humans throughout history, as it has made both huge contributions and disasters to our civilization. In the second decade of the 21st century, the metaphor of fire may extend to the crisis at Japan's Fukushima Daiichi Nuclear Power Plant in March, 2011,[43] a plant that provided prosperity and convenient life-style as well as disasters to the residents of the archipelago.

The end of the story around Izanagi and Izanami was tragic and sorrowful. However, many modern readers will feel little sympathy toward them due to their barbaric behaviors, selfishness, lack of morality and compassion toward their own children. Furthermore, the behavior of Izanagi's children were even worse than their father, and they acted no better than serial killers in today's world. In a sense, Hiruko was

---

41   Wikipedia: Prometheus. Online at http://en.wikipedia.org/wiki/Prometheus
42   Kenneth C. Davis. Don't know Much About Mythology. (New York, USA: HarperCollins Publisher, 2005) p. 387
43   Wikipedia: Fukushima Daiichi Nuclear Power Plant. Online at http://en.wikipedia.org/wiki/Fukushima_Daiichi_Nuclear_Power_Plant

more fortunate than his younger siblings because he was abandoned as a child and therefore had no chance to inherit the violent and anti-social personality from his father. Later, he was raised by a fisher named Ebisu Saburo with much better quality of life with him than his original father, and eventually became the Ebisu god, one of the *Seven deities of good fortune*. Because he was separated from his violent father, he had the privilege to join a group of civilized deities, while all of siblings remained savage.

The crudeness and barbarism of the Japanese mythological progenitors also have close parallels to similar behaviors of Greek deities and heroes. The primitive Japan was an illiterate and barbaric society like many other nations on this planet, a far cry from both Judeo-Christian ethics and the moral standard of secular society of the 21st century.

Because of this, Haiyama's (1996)[44] assumption that the ancient Japanese was as bloody as the populations of other parts of the world of the same days is easily understood. The ancient Japanese sacrificed human subjects in their religious ceremonies and consumed human flesh, especially sexual organs to increase fertility, just like those in China and the Middle East. However, these practices had been long forgotten because there were no written documents to support them.

It is safe to conclude that the lack of the morals and extremely crude way of life was universally prevalent all over the world prior to the Seventh Century, and most humans on this planet lived savagely. Modern ethical principles based on the Judeo-Christian tradition which emphasis on the dignity and equality of all mankind, compassion to the children, poor

---

44   Haiyama, ibid

and needy, was foreign to a vast majority that lived in the antiquity. It seems unrealistic to expect simple, illiterate and unlearned nations, which lived in the ancient times, to have more civilized and sophisticated behaviour and code of ethics like those who live in the modern world.

Furthermore, Japanese, prior to the introduction of Buddhism around the Seventh Century seemed to have little hope in their afterlife. According to the primitive Shinto, death was nothing more than a curse, a misfortune and unclean event. The early Japanese had the concept that the souls of the dead are expected to go to the dark afterlife, the Land of Yomi, or a hopeless place like Hades regardless of one's conduct during one's lifetime. It was a horrendous place where even a beautiful woman like Izanami was transformed into a hideous monster. It is no wonder that most people started conducting funerals in Buddhist temples as soon as the Buddhism was introduced to the nation from China.

Sarutahiho Ōkami

Sarutahiko is one of the significant deities in the foundational story of the early Shinto. He is a powerful guardian kami who is enshrined at *Sarutahiko Shrine* (猿田彦神社)[45] and Tsubaki Grand Shrine (椿大神社)[46] in *Mie* Prefecture and 2,000 other shrines all over the country. He plays an important role in Kojiki although he is an earthly deity and not a part of the Amaterasu family. In the Kojiki, he is the leader of local deity and the one who led Prince Ninigi, the grandson of Amaterasu, the Sun goddess, when he descended

---

45   Wikipedia: 猿田彦神社. Online at http://ja.wikipedia.org/wiki/%E7%8C%BF%E7%94%B0%E5%BD%A6%E7%A5%9E%E7%A4%BE

46   Wikipedia: Tsubaki Grand Shrine. Online at http://en.wikipedia.org/wiki/Tsubaki_Grand_Shrine

from Takamagahara. His name is traditionally transcribed with the character (猿田) that signifies the meaning "monkey-field" followed by the Classical Japanese noun "hiko" or "a male child of noble blood, a prince." However, his appearance with a big long nose resembles Tengu[47] (天狗) or "heavenly dogs," one of the supernatural creatures found in Japanese folklore and legends, rather than a monkey.

In one story, Prince Ninigi comes to earth with the command of Queen Amaterasu, and lands at the middle of a field filled with reeds of Takamagahara. Then, Sarutahiko, a local kami, is standing in the midst of the sky shining at the center of the Milky Way. There is also a female kami who serves Amaterasu standing in the space and illuminates the "field of the high sky" in the heavenly realm and illuminates the land of Ashihara beneath her. Her name is Ameno-uzume- no-mikoto or Uzume, and Amaterasu said to her, "You must ask his name because you are a brave goddess, although you have an appearance of a weak woman".

Uzume is a heavenly dancer known for boldness and sexually provocative behaviors, and often reveals her breasts and privates in public. She asks him, "Who are you that blocks the center of the way where our Imperial son is about to come and descend to Earth?" Then, the god shining at the galaxy with his glowing exterior responds, "I am a local deity named Sarutahiko. I visited you to have the honor to be the guide of your royal prince, since I heard that the Imperial son of Sun goddess Amaterasu is going to descend to Earth".

After introducing himself, Sarutahiko guides Prince Ninigi and his entire troop to the best location to land and

---

47   Wikipedia: Tengu. Online at http://en.wikipedia.org/wiki/Tengu

settle. He marries Uzume who initiates a conversation with him after this incident. Like all other Shinto kami, Sarutahiko had vulnerability in his flesh, so that he eventually dies being bitten by a shellfish while fishing in the sea. This incident could indicate that he died during sexual intercourse with Uzume or some other woman, because in ancient Japanese the term "shellfish" was a euphemism for female genitalia. The expression "fishing in the sea" could also indicate an activity related to a sexual activity, since the term "sea" universally illustrates human sexuality according to Jungian psycho-analysis[48]. D. H. Lawrence (1885–1930)[49] used the term "sea of life" to illustrate sexual activities in his novel *Lady Chatterley's Lover* (1960)[50]. Therefore, some modern Japanese writers often speculate the cause of his death was a stroke or heart attack during intercourse or due to a sexually transmitted disease.

Later, Sarutahiko was enshrined as a god in Tsubaki Grand Shrine, Sarutahiko Srrine in Mie prefecture and many other Shinto shrines all over the country. Thereafter, he is considered as a powerful and very significant guardian kami who led a divine royal prince to Earth in the Shinto tradition. He is also considered as a god of crossroads, pathways and surmounting obstacles, who protects travelers from enemies and ruthless nature, since he guided Ninigi to land on Earth. There is a question regarding when and why Sarutahiko was enshrined as a god in these shrines. In Shinto, many mortals are enshrined and become gods upon death. However,

---

48   Carl Gustav Jung. Man and His Symbols. (NY, USA: Dell Publishing, 1968)
49   Wikipedia: D. H. Lawrence. Online at http://en.wikipedia.org/wiki/D._H._Lawrence
50   D. H. Lawrence. Lady Chatterley's Lover. (MT, USA: Kessinger Publishing, LLC, 1960/2010)

Sarutahiko was already kami or deity during his lifetime. Therefore, unlike mortals, his enshrinement did not mean deification or becoming a god. There is another question if there was a real historical person who Sarutahiko was modeled after just like Heracles[51] in Greek myth. Some even speculate that if he were a real person in human history he could have either Indian or European heritage, since he had an exceptionally long nose.

It is interesting that in Osamu Tezuka's (1928-1989)[52] Phoenix (1967),[53] both Sarutahiko and Uzume appear as real persons in Japanese history. The story consists of various periods of human history including the future or the space age. The first two stoies of the Phoenix series are loosely based on Kojiki and Nihonshoki or a demythologized version of the most archaic Japanese twin narratives.

In Tezuka's story, Sarutahiko was a general who served Queen Himiko[54] (d. ca. 248), a legendary and obscure shaman queen. Sarutahiko's nose was not hereditary, but a result of punishment by the queen for his disobedience. Uzume is also an actual person who mates Sarutahiko very briefly and produces offspring after his death. She is a beautiful woman who serves Emperor Jimmu, coming from either China or Korea to conquer the land of Yamato, but disguised in the appearance of an ugly woman to keep away soldiers in the army. Uzume asks Sarutahiko to mate her when he is captured by Jimmu, but he refuses because he thinks she is the ugliest woman he ever met. However, he accepts her offer after

51   Wikipedia: Heracles. Online at http://en.wikipedia.org/wiki/Heracles
52   Wikipedia: Osamu Tezuka. Online at http://en.wikipedia.org/wiki/Tezuka
53   Wikipedia: Phoenix (manga). Online at http://en.wikipedia.org/wiki/Phoenix_ (manga)
54   Wikipedia: Himiko. Online at http://en.wikipedia.org/wiki/Himiko

he discovers how beautiful she really is. Shortly after this, Sarutahiko escapes from Jimmu's camp, returns to the nation of Yamatai to which he belongs. Jimmu, the grandson of Ninigi, a legendary warrior emperor in Japanese mythology, forces Sarutahiko to guide the troops to Yamatai. However, contrary to the myth, he refuses to do so and fights against them. He finally dies defending Yamatai from Jimmu's invasion force. After his death, Uzume discloses the fact that she already has conceived his child.

Tezuka's story, which describes Sarutahiko as a hero who fought against the ancient imperial troops instead of for them, may indicate the author's philosophy of disapproval of the Kokutai or emperor centered cultic community and the State Shinto prior to the Second World War. The story describes Sarutahiko as a general of Yamatai, who fiercely fought the invasion troops of the Emperor Jimmu who emigrated from the continent. Yamatai, the indigenous Japanese tribal nation, was technologically inferior to the Imperial force from the continent. Jimmu's troops had horses and more advanced weapons than the indigenous Japanese.

After the Yamatai force exhausted all their military resources, the General received more than ten arrows in his body and bled to death. Shortly after, Uzume, who arrived following Jimmu's troops, saw Sarutahiko's body and told him that he is not a loser, since he now has offspring. Tezuka made one of the significant deities in the ancient myth a hero who fought against the troops of Jimmu the divine warrior emperor, according to the tradition of the State Shinto created in the Meiji era by the oligarchy and government leaders. He did so likely because he was repulsed with State Shinto and the atmosphere of Imperial Japan before the Second World War, in which he spent his childhood and youth. The totalitarian regime forced him to believe an absurd teaching based on the myth that the Japanese emperor was a sacred demigod descended from an unbroken lineage from the sun-goddess Amaterasu.

In Tezuka's story, the descendants of the couple with the same long nose are depicted throughout the history of mankind. Some of them end up with a long nose as a punishment or a disaster they encounter as their ancestors did. However, some others like Dr. Saruta who witnesses the end of mankind, possess a hereditary long nose. In the series, those in the later age tend to have hereditary long noses. Readers may speculate that this was due to mixed marriages of the descendents with non-Japanese. The main theme of Phoenix is the reincarnation or transmigration of souls throughout millennia. However, the storyline doesn't clearly indicate if they are simply the offspring of Sarutahiko or his reincarnated identities.

According to the legend based on Kojiki and Nihonshoki, Sarutahiko and Uzume also had human offspring during their lifetime. There are many people in Japan whose family name is Saruta (猿田) and they follow the tradition that they are descended from the divine progenitor. Many others with different family names also follow the tradition that they are descended from the patriarch with a long nose.

The chief priest in both Tsubaki Grand Shrine and Sarutahiko Srrine and many others all over Japan claimed that they were descended from the ancient couple. In Greek mythology, an offspring of two divine parents is fully divine and only one divine parent is half divine. The only exception was Dionysus,[55] the god of the grape harvest, and wine, a son of Zeus and the mortal woman Semele, but fully divine. However, in Japanese counterpart, there is no such rule. Sometimes, full deity is born when only one of the parents is divine, and a mortal human child is born when both parents are divine. Therefore, it was not strange that all of Sarutahiko's children were considered mortals although both of their parents were deities.

Ōkuninushi

[56]Ōkuninushi (大国主)[57] or Great Country Lord is another significant Kami in Shinto legend according to Kojiki and Nihonshoki. The literal meaning of his name is "Great Land Master", but he has many different names. Regarding his identity and personal history, Kojiki and Nihonshoki have different viewpoints. He was originally the ruler of Izumo Province, and Susa-no-Ō's son according to the main part of Nihonshoki. However, Kojiki and a small portion of Nihonshoki stated that he was a sixth generation descendent of Susa-no-Ō. Later, Ōkuninushi retired from the position as the chief deity of Izumo Province, and Ninigi, the progenitor of the Japanese imperial family took over the job. After that, he was given a position to rule the unseen world of spirits and magic in compensation. He was also considered a god of nation-building, farming, business, and medicine according to the Shinto tradition.

---

55   Wikipedia: Dionysus. Online at http://en.wikipedia.org/wiki/Bacchus
56   Wikipedia: Ōkuninushi. Online at http://en.wikipedia.org/wiki/%C5%8Ckuninushi
57   Wikipedia: 大国主. Online at http://ja.wikipedia.org/wiki/%E5%A4%A7%E5%9B%BD%E4%B8%BB

The discrepancies between documents regarding the identity of Ōkuninushi illustrate his obscure origin. Anna Andreeva (2006) suggests that the obscure identity of the deity may indicate his Korean origin. She contends that Ōkuninushi's origins are a composite of many deities of Izumo, possibly worshipped by Korean immigrants, but were forgotten and abandoned, and received little mention in the official records[58]. During Yayoi period, there were many influences and a massive immigration of people from Korea. These immigrants from the Korean peninsula introduced the primitive nation to new deities as well as to iron, new weapons and agricultural tools. The new gods introduced gradually integrated themselves into the Shinto tradition passed by from the Jomon period. Generally speaking, many deities in the Izumo Province were originally worshiped by Koreans, who immigrated to Japan during the Yayoi period. On the other hand, gods from Yamato Province were predominantly indigenous Kami coming from Proto-Shinto tradition during Jomon period. Most scholars now agree that Ōkuninushi belongs to the former.

Like most other Shinto Kami, Ōkuninushi had many wives and produced numerous descendents. His first wife was Princess Yakami (八上比売), a prize woman whom he won after fighting 80 other brothers who wanted to marry her. After he married Yakami, his furious brothers murdered him twice. The first time, he managed to come back to life because his mother Sashikuni-Wakahime (刺国若姫) revived him. However, when they crushed Ōkuninushi to death the second time, his mother advised him to take refuge in the underworld, or Land of Yomi, ruled by Susa-no-Ō.

---

58   Anna Andreeva. Saidaiji Monks and Esoteric Kami Worship at Ise and Miwa. Japanese Journal of Religious Studies, 2006. 349-377

His second wife was Suseri-Hime (須勢理毘売命)[59], a daughter of Susa-no-Ō with whom he fell in love with shortly after visiting the underworld. Shortly after they wed, Suseri-Hime introduced Ōkuninushi to her father. One of the meanest deities in Japanese myth, Susa-no-Ō was aghast and furious when he knew the relationship between the two. He sent Ōkuninushi to sleep in a room full of snakes. However, the bride saved him by given him a scarf with a spell to keep away the snakes. Then the next night, Susa-no-Ō sent the groom to a room filled with centipedes and wasps. However, Suseri-Hime protected him again by giving him nuts and clay to show an appearance that he had smashed one of the centipedes and gave them fear. After giving him a series of trials, Susa-no-Ō finally began to approve of Ōkuninushi as his daughter's groom. When Ōkuninushi passed the last test by successfully arriving at the border of the underworld accompanying his bride, Susa-no-Ō gave him powerful weapons, and advised him to fight his brothers before returning to the land of the living[60].

As mentioned, prior to meeting Suseri-Hime in the underworld, Ōkuninushi had already married to the princess Yakami. Yakami didn't try to compete with his new bride and went back to her parents' home, leaving a baby son Kinomata to her husband. Yakami did not fight since she knew that Suseri-Hime was far more powerful than herself. Ōkuninushi also gave up on her despite having battled 80 warriors for her and because of his new bride. Kinomata, (木俣神)[61] his first son with Yakami, was the Kami of the tree, well and stream,

59   Wikipedia: スセリビメ. Online at http://ja.wikipedia.org/wiki/%E3%82%B9%E3
%82%BB%E3%83%AA%E3%83%93%E3%83%A1
60   Wikipedia: Ōkuninushi. ibid.
61   Wikipedia: 木俣神. Online at http://ja.wikipedia.org/wiki/%E6%9C%A8%E4%BF
%A3%E7%A5%9E

according to the legend. Although abandoned by his mother as an infant, he grew up to be a kind and graceful deity with a pure heart. The legend also said that he created many wells across the country and helped people by providing water[62]. Kinomata appears to be a deity to administrate the basic necessity of mankind because we need both water and oxygen produced by trees.

The animated fantasy musical film, *Corpse Bride* (2005), produced by Tim Burton, has a close parallel with the story of Ōkuninushi and Suseri-Hime in Kojiki and Nihonshoki, since the animated musical conceives the motif of romance between a man from the world of living and a beautiful woman from the underworld[63]. The story setting is a late Victorian Era European village. A son of a rich fish merchant named Victor Van Dort was betrothed to Victoria Everglot, a daughter of aristocrats and preparing for an arranged marriage. The two fall in love when they first met although they worried about marrying someone they did not know. Victor was so shy and clumsy that he ruined the wedding rehearsal. So he practiced his wedding vows in a nearby forest because he is determined to do better in the wedding itself. When he placed the wedding ring on a nearby upturned tree root, it turns out to be the finger of a dead beautiful woman clad in a bridal gown, and she now claimed Victor's wife.

Whisked away to the Land of the Dead, Victor learns the story of Emily who was murdered by her fiancé years ago on the night of her secret elopement. After Victor has a failed attempt to escape from Emily, he becomes more sympathetic

---

62   木俣神（きのまたのかみ）:夢神社, 2011. Online at http://210.166.216.200/original/otokogami/detail.php?id=32

63   Wikipedia: Corpse Bride. Online at http://en.wikipedia.org/wiki/Corpse_Bride

to her. Meanwhile, he also learns that Victoria is about to marry Lord Barkis, a wicked aristocrat. Victor makes a decision to terminate his life and join Emily, since he has nothing to keep him in the world of living. The wedding takes place in the world of livings because Victor is still alive. He is going to take a cup of poison when he vows marriage to his bride. However, they encounter those from the living world including Victoria and Lord Barkis who was Emily's former fiancé who murdered her for her dowry. Emily stops Victor from ending his life and asks him to stay with Victoria. Emily releases the young man from his vow to marry her, returning the wedding ring to him. As she steps into the moonlight from the church after blessing Victor and Victoria, Emily finds eternal peace. Since her killer is finally punished, she can rest in peace.

Both Suseri-Hime and Emily are eerie, but attractive, women who live in the underworld and are deeply in love with younger men from the world of the living. However, one is a powerful goddess and a daughter of Susa-no-Ō, the ruler of Hades, while the other is a human ghost murdered by her fiancé. However, as a ghost she can exercise a considerable amount of power over the living. When Victor lies to her and visits Victoria instead of his parents, she is immediately snatched back to the underworld. Both stories carry the theme of a death wish and necrophilia among those who are tired of life in the world of living. For the one who is disappointed with life and has lost the will to live, death could be a beautiful and sweet lover. At the end of the story, Victor Van Dort safely escapes the underworld and returns to the world of the living as does Ōkuninushi. Both Ōkuninushi who was murdered by his older siblings and Victor who lost his beloved Victoria agree to marry the underworld beauty. However, unlike a Shinto Kami, Victor returns to his original bride from the world of living. He likely could return to Victoria since he was still alive when he went to the underworld and was not yet married to Emily. At the same time Emily was simply a human ghost murdered by her evil fiancé, while Suseri-Hime was a furious female deity who would never release her man to the first wife.

The termination of the marriage between Ōkuninushi and his first wife Yakami is supported by both Shinto and Buddhist tradition in that he died once and went down to the underworld. Nevertheless, in Japanese traditional thinking, there is also a popular belief that a marriage may last even beyond the grave, contrary to the Shinto and Buddhist doctrines. Because of this, there is a custom even now that a husband and wife are buried in the same tomb so that they reunite when both are dead. However, it was a concept developed in the mediaeval period. Both the primitive Shinto and original Buddhism supported the view that death ends the marriage relationship the same as Christian belief. The union between the dead and living is absolutely taboo in all three religious traditions. Following the Christian tradition, Emily would not be able to join her prospective groom until his life was terminated.

Unlike Ōkuninushi, Victor still belongs to the realm of the living throughout the story. Therefore, it is safe to conclude that the largest reason that Victor could reunite with his original bride, unlike the Shinto Kami, is that he was still alive when he travelled to the underworld.

Ōkuninushi was able to travel back to the realm of living and lived there again with his new bride from the underworld even after his death because he was a deity. However, Victor, as a mere human, could never live among the living once he is dead. Although Shinto deities from Kojiki and Nihonshoki were more vulnerable than gods from other mythologies like Chronos and Zeus, they had many privileges that mortal humans do not possess. One of their privileges that mortals do not have was an easy access to travel around many different realms of the universe including the heavens, earth and underworld.

Yamato Takeru

The last and most significant hero in Kojiki and Nihonshoki is [64]Yamato Takeru (日本武尊, やまとたける)[65], a legendary warrior prince of the Yamato dynasty. He is a son of Emperor Keikō, a legendary monarch who is counted as the 12th Emperor of Japan according to tradition. However, most historians do not believe in the existence of either Yamato Takeru or his father Emperor Keikō. Nevertheless, there is a possibility that the character of Yamato Takeru was modeled after several different individuals who did exist and then went through the process of modifications throughout the ages. Richard Hornby (2008) contends that the legend of Yamato Takeru is known as a *Kabuki* story and was popularized among commoners after the Edo Period[66].

Probably, the historical background of this legend is somehow between the Yayoi and Kofun periods (古墳時代: 250 - 538)[67] when males increased their value due to their physical

64   Wikipedia: Yamato Takeru. Online at http://en.wikipedia.org/wiki/Yamato_Takeru
65   Wikipedia: ヤマトタケル. Online at http://ja.wikipedia.org/wiki/%E3%83%A4%E3%83%9E%E3%83%88%E3%82%BF%E3%82%B1%E3%83%AB
66   Richard Hornby. Kabuki Goes Hollywood The Hudson Review: Volume LXI, Number 3, 2008. 516-522
67   Wikipedia: Kofun period. Online at http://en.wikipedia.org/wiki/Kofun_period

strength to fight in a battle and work in agriculture in the paddy fields. Wars between tribes became more prevalent than the previous era because of the introduction of iron and more advanced weapons. The iron also provided residents more advanced agricultural tools and the opportunity to exit from the primitive lifestyle of hunting and gathering. However, the farming during this era required more intense labor than the previous era. Yamato Takeru might well represent the image of the most ideal man among those who lived in Japan during the Yayoi period which required powerful, mighty warriors.

The Kofun period which followed the Yayoi period is considered the oldest era of recorded history in Japan. The term *kofun* (古墳) is a Japanese word referring to burial mounds dating from this era. During this era, people in Japan imported and developed the custom of building burial mounds for rulers that there were great signs of the arrival of more advanced architecture and a writing system from the continent. Also, the chief of the Yamato tribe started calling himself the king during the Kofun period and helped his people become the most powerful and dominant group of the country, and eventually claimed himself the emperorship of the nation in the following period.

Unlike the most other heroes in the twin narratives, Yamato Takeru was considered fully human and mortal, since neither of his parents was a deity. However, according to the legend, he had some divine attributes like Heracles[68] in the Greek myth, and was well known for an extraordinary physical strength and military prowess as a mortal. In fact, unlike Heracles, both of his parents were humans. However,

68   Wikipedia: Heracles. Online at http://en.wikipedia.org/wiki/Heracles

he was considered semi-divine because he was a part of the royal family descended from an unbroken lineage from the sun-goddess Amaterasu. Like all other divine heroes in Kojiki and Nihonshoki, Takeru could use supernatural force. His supernatural power was mostly coming from his holy sword, one of his family treasures from Susa-no-Ō. The sword was passed through generations and Takeru obtained it from his aunt and Shinto high-priestess Yamatohime.

There are several differences between Kojiki and Nihonshoki regarding the character of Yamato Takeru and his storyline. For instance, Prince Ousu (小碓命 – Takeru's childhood name) slew his twin brother Ōusu (大碓命) and his father feared his brutal temperament, according to Kojiki. However, Nihonshoki never mentions this incident. The brutal side of Takeru is comparable to Samson[69] in the Old Testament and Siegfried[70] in the Norse Myth. In fact, in antiquity, there were many heroes with extremely cruel, cold-blooded characters without ordinary human emotions in myths from various parts of the world. Perhaps, it was because many prehistoric nations lived in a perpetual state of war, and were forced to kill and destroy those from opposing nations for survival. These people groups in prehistory could not afford to possess the 21st century's standard mindset.

Regarding the difference between the two narratives, Kojiki described Takeru in a conflicting relationship with the emperor who was his father. The emperor feared the brutal temperament of young Ousu and therefore sent him on a mission to conquer the land of Kumaso, hoping he might be killed in battle. However, according to Nihonshoki, he was the

---

69   Judges 13-16.
70   Wikipedia: Siegfried. Online at http://en.wikipedia.org/wiki/Siegfried_(opera)

consistently loyal and beloved son of the Emperor Keikō, and his appointed heir. Therefore, upon his death, the emperor greatly grieved since he lost his mightiest heir and had to appoint his younger son Prince Wakatarashihiko who was without physical strength, military prowess or intelligence, but had an ordinary personality and weaker character. Later, Wakatarashihiko became Emperor Seimu and lived to be 95, according to Kojiki and 107 according to Nihonshoki. According to legend, Seimu had a deep awe and respect for his older brother Yamato Takeru, so that he appointed Tarashinakatsuhiko, his nephew and Takeru's son as the heir to be Emperor Chuai instead of one of his sons.

However, Yamato Takeru had a softer and more sensitive side than most legendary, prehistoric heroes as well as a brutal character. For instance, he deeply lamented and expressed sorrow when he lost his wife Ototachibanahime (弟橘媛) during a storm. She was the most beloved among his wives, and she jumped into a roaring sea storm and sacrificed her life to sooth the rage of the sea god in order to save the life of her husband and his troops. Upon his death, he also expressed a deep longing for Yamato, the native land where he grew up. This could be because the story of Yamato Takeru came from the memory of the illiterate and barbaric era through oral tradition, yet was compiled as literature in a more cultured age.

Before the end of the Seventh Century, Japan made a dramatic transition from a mere collection of barbaric tribes into an established nation-state with a centralized government[71]. It abandoned the savage day's life style and sealed off the memory of Proto-Shinto religious practices

---

71   Isao Ebihara. Shinto War Gods of Yasukuni Shrine. (Dayton, TN: USA: Global Ed Advance, 2011)

including cannibalism and human sacrifice, which did not fit the newly acquired image as a civilized nation. The leaders during the era were extremely eager to acquire the literacy and knowledge from China, including new technology, writing system and a state-governing system based on Taoism, Confucianism and Buddhism. The original story of Yamato Takeru was coming from the barbaric era before the import of the writing system and Chinese philosophies. It is possible that the writers of Kojiki and Nihonshoki modified the heroic epoch of Yamato Takeru to fit into a more civilized nation. However, there was no evidence of modifications to the original story because Japan prior to the Seventh Century illiterate society. When these narratives were released, the original story came from the oral transmission only after the illiterate era had died out.

Thomas P Kaslis[72] notes that these two chronicles contained the different roles that the Japanese court officials intended. According to him, *Nihonshoki* was originally written in Chinese because it was designed to present to foreign readers as an authoritative document about Japanese culture, history and its religio-political foundations. In keeping with the new focus, Nihonshoki, the second written chronicle of the island nation, does not include the discourse that Takeru slaughters his brother Ōusu or the most brutal parts of the story. This was written slightly after Kojiki, and the target readers were Chinese diplomats instead of Japanese natives. We could easily speculate that the writers of the second literature eliminated the most brutish and inhumane part of the legend in order to impress Chinese government officials. At the same

---

72   Thomas P Kasulis. Shinto --- The Way Home (Honolulu, HI: USA: University of Hawaii Press, 2004)

time, Nihonshoki describes Emperor Keikō, Takeru's father, as a more graceful and refined person than in the first narrative. Kojiki, on the other hand, describes the emperor as a mean person who attempted to kill his son several times out of fear of his extraordinary physical strength and military prowess, but Nihonshoki never mentions it.

This shows the strong possibility that writers of Kojiki and Nihonshoki belong to different circles. Kojiki fervently pursed the aesthetics of the literature and attempted to entice the interest of readers. On the other hand, Nihonshoki tended to be dry and boring as literature and overly concerned with political correctness. Quite possibly the writers of the second narrative were rigid bureaucrats who simply followed the policy of the governments, or imperial loyalists who denied anything wrong in the family.

On the other hand, Kojiki was compiled by a group led by leading scholar Hieda no Are[73], who had a more liberal and honest description regarding the monarchy or the ruling family of the whole nation, since the target readers were Japanese nationals. According to Kaslis, Kojiki was directed to Japanese readers and was, at least in part, a cultural preservation project. The writers must have intended to use Kojiki to educate and edify the Japanese public that was still predominantly illiterate and undereducated[74].

At the same time, it is not difficult to conclude that writers of Nihonshoki intentionally sent a subliminal message that Japan had transformed into a more civilized nation-state and no longer lived as savages. In fact, Japan around the Seventh

---

73   Wikipedia: Hieda no Are稗田阿礼. Online at http://en.wikipedia.org/wiki/Hieda_no_Are
74   Ebihara. Shinto War Gods of Yasukuni Shrine. ibid.

Century was desperately seeking for support and recognition from China. After the completion of Kojiki, the government officials discovered that they might need another document to convince China that their nation was out of the savage era.

Yamato Takeru & Evil Twin Motif

According to Kojiki Prince Ōusu, Takeru's twin brother was an evil and delinquent character who slept with one of his father's queens and didn't show up to the family meal at all. Then, the father sent Prince Ousu to tell his brother to come to the family meal, and teach him a lesson if he refused to do so. He obeyed his father and taught his brother a lesson, but in a little too harsh way. He squeezed Ōusu to death with his mighty hands and ripped limbs off from his body and threw them out.

The Kojiki discourse regarding Ousu slaying his brother Ōusu (大碓命) might be an archaic example of the evil twin motif that is prevalent in novels, movies in theatres, TV series, anime and manga series. A discourse that a protagonist or some other significant character has a conflicting relationship with an evil twin until finally killing him is a very important developmental motif of Jungian archetype theory. In this sense, every individual has an evil twin, and must kill him or her to grow or pass into a very significant maturation process.

For instance, in Star Trek: The Next Generation, a popular sci-fi TV series in 1990s, an android character named Data has an evil twin similar to Yamato Takeru whose name is Lore. [75] Data is a Starfleet officer and Soong-type android equipped with a sophisticated positronic brain. The androids look like identical twins because they were modeled after Dr. Noonian Soong, who designed them. Both Data and Lore have extremely

---

75   MemoryAlpha:Lore, 2011. Online at http://memory-alpha.org/wiki/Lore

advanced brains and were sentient, possessed superior strength, speed and intelligence when compared to a human. However, Lore who was constructed slightly earlier than Data and began displaying signs of emotional instability and anti-social behaviors, leading him to see himself as superior to humans. He eventually wreaked havoc on the Omicron Theta colony by contacting Crystalline Entity, a powerful, space-borne creature, and killed all residents there. Soong captured, deactivated and dismantled him shortly before the Crystalline Entity destroyed the colony. Lore stayed inactive for decades until the Starfleet discovered and activated him when they searched the ruins of Omicron Theta colony.

Shortly before the colony was destroyed by the Crystalline Entity, Soong constructed another android named Data without destabilizing emotions like Lore. Later, the Starfleet officers discovered Data in the ruins and activated him. He was educated in the Starfleet Academy and became an officer after graduating from the academy. He was then assigned to the Starship Enterprise and this character became a regular member of *Star Trek: The Next Generation*. Data was as intelligent as Lore because he had the same level of sophistication in his positronic brain, although his metrics had minor differences from his brother. However, he lacked the capability to feel emotions, since his father Dr. Noonian Soong feared the possibility that his emotions might fail and subsequently develop an evil character like his brother.

After Lore was reactivated by a group of Starfleet officers who visited the ruins of Omicron Theta colony, Data encountered Lore several times, and had a conflicting relationship with him. Later, Noonian created an emotion chip for Data that would allow him to feel human emotions, but Lore tricked Soong, posed as his brother and stole it. Later, Lore modified the new emotion chip and used it to feed Data negative emotions from distance and manipulate him. The negative emotions coming from Lore disabled Data's ethical program, but he finally overcame it and restored his sense of right and wrong. Data fired upon Lore and deactivated him, whose last words were "I love you brother". Lore's body was disassembled by the Starfleet and the emotion chip was removed and returned to its intended owner.

In Jungian psychoanalytical language, it was an extremely important event for Data, since he finally obtained an ability to feel human emotions by deactivating his evil twin and taking the emotion chip from him. His newly obtained emotions were perfect and not unstable like Lore. Thus, the symbolic event to slay an evil twin sibling was a universally significant developmental process that every individual must experience sometime in his or her life. In the same way, in Kojiki, young Ousu slaughtered his evil twin brother Ōusu. It was a significant initiation ceremony upon which young Ousu, whose name signifies "little prince," became the legendary great warrior Yamato Takeru. It was an important developmental step to kill a demon within by overcoming conflicting self images - the discrepancy between real and ideal egos according to Jung.

Richard Hornby maintains that in a Kabuki show, the roles of both Ousu and Ōusu were played by the same actor Ichikawa Danjiro (b.1946)[76]. The actor differentiated the two characters by dressing Ousu in a magnificent white costume with gold

76   Wikipedia: 市川團十郎 (12代目). Online at http://ja.wikipedia.org/wiki/%E5%B8%82%E5%B7%9D%E5%9C%98%E5%8D%81%E9%83%8E_(12%E4%BB%A3%E7%9B%AE)

trim and Ōusu all in black.[77] The play in which the same actor played twin brothers might eloquently illustrate a significant initiation ceremony in the developmental process of a person to kill a demon within. Likewise, in StarTrek:TNG, both Data and Lore were played by the same actor Brent Spiner (b.1949)[78].

Military Campaign to Kumaso

Prince Ousu made many military campaigns to conquer tribal nations in various regions of Japan during his short life and received renowned fame and admiration as the greatest hero in Japan throughout the ages. After killing his brother Ōusu, the emperor ordered him to travel to the land of Kumaso and conquer the tribal nation there. After he invaded Kumaso, he slew Kawakami Takeru, the local chief. Upon his death, the Kumaso chief praised the military prowess of the young prince and gave him the name Takeru which means a great warrior. Then, he was named Yamato Takeru, which means the great warrior of the land of Yamato. It was the second important initiation ceremony for him, because he took not only the name but strength from Kumaso's chief.

The discourse that young Ousu became Yamato Takeru by killing Kawakami Takeru, another great warrior of his days, might also imply the ceremonial rite of cannibalism coming from the most archaic memory of the island nation. According to Haiyama (1996)[79], Proto-Shinto carried the belief that one could absorb strength, physical or intellectual power by consuming the flesh or body parts of others mightier than him or her. He suggested the possibility that the Proto-Japanese tribal warriors often consumed penis, brain and other vital

---

77   Hornby. Ibid.
78   Wikipedia: Brent Spiner. Online at http://en.wikipedia.org/wiki/Brent_Spiner
79   Haiyama. ibid.

organs of the defeated enemies to accumulate the power and become stronger and mightier.

Klingons[80] in the fictional Star Trek universe are known for consuming the heart taken out of the slaughtered enemies' bodies while it is still warm and moving. For a Klingon, it is also considered honorable to be slain and have your heart consumed by a mighty warrior. It is generally considered that the Klingons adhered to a strict code of honor similar to feudal Japanese customs[81]. However, the custom of eating the slain enemies' heart seems to have stemmed from the Proto-Shinto during the Jomon period or the most archaic part of the collective unconscious memory of the barbaric past of all mankind rather than feudal Japanese customs.

This is also reminiscent of Highlander,[82] a popular fantasy action film in theatre and TV in the 1990s. It was a story of an immortal Scottish warrior named Connor MacLeod and his great nephew Duncan. Both Connor and Duncan were over 400 years old, but didn't look older than their 30s. The immortal warriors of this series could not die, unless decapitated by an opponent. When they lose their head, they would experience lightening and thunder and a pulse of energy called "quickening". When the winner received quickening coming from his or her dead opponent, this person obtained power from the dead and increased his strength. This series seems to follow the idea of the prehistoric cannibalism, in which one increased one's power by eating the flesh of a dead hero. In this case, thunder like "quickening" or a pulse of

---

80   Wikipedia: Klingon culture. Online at http://en.wikipedia.org/wiki/Klingon_culture
81   Wikipedia: Klingon. Online at http://en.wikipedia.org/wiki/Klingon
82   Wikipedia: Highlander (film). Online at http://en.wikipedia.org/wiki/Highlander_(film)

energy coming out of the dead body replaces real human flesh to be consumed during the ceremonial rite.

Military Campaign to Ezo

Yamato Takeru also made a great campaign to conquer the land of Ezo, the northern part of Japan. The tribal leaders of Ezo district were heavily guarded and protected by the shamanic power of the local priests or priestess. However, Takeru's spiritual force overpowered local shamans, so that his troops could conquer the district without using arms. Toshihiko Moriya (1968)[83] maintains that Takeru's troops included a person with extraordinary magical power. Moriya contends that the person must be Ototachibanahime, his most beloved wife who sacrificed her life to sooth the rage of the sea god to save him and his men.

The origin and full identity of Ototachibanahime has been long debated, but scholars and writers have not yet reached a united conclusion. Some say she is a daughter of a fisher or farmer from a very humble background, and some others state she is to be part of the royal family of Yamato and related to Takeru. Aritsune Toyota (b. 1938), a Japanese creative writer, wrote a series of stories of Yamato Takeru in 1970s. According to his story, Ototachibanahime was a foreign princess from an Indian royal family. While she was drifting in the sea after a long voyage from India, Takeru rescued her and made her his wife[84].

Nevertheless, Moriya maintains that she was at least a woman with a shamanic function, particularly a power to sooth

---

83   Toshihiko Moriya. Yamato Takeru Densho Josetsu [Introduction to Yamato Takeru Legend]. (Osaka: Izumi Shoin, 1968)
84   Aritsune Toyota. Hinokuni no Yamato Takeru [Yamato Takeru in the Land of Fire]. (Tokyo: Shodensha, 1971)

deities in the sea. There is a general consensus that although her origin and full identity was not revealed in Kojiki and Nihonshoki and she remains a mystery, she must be a woman with extraordinary magical and shamanic power who aided the hero by creating more advantageous conditions in battle. If she were an Indian royal princess as in Toyota's story, she must belong to the class of Brahmin with unusual spiritual force and the ultimate authority over interpretation of Vedic and Puranic sacred texts like the Vedas, Upanishads and Bhagavad-Gita[85]. The idea that Ototachibanahime was originally an Indian princess is entertaining, but those in academic circles consider this a historically challenged view. Though Toyota's story was a stretch from the historians' perspectives, the Brahmin background of the princess would well qualify her as a shamaness or supernatural aid to assist the great hero in battles.

Death of Yamato Takeru

As mentioned, Yamato Takeru grieved greatly at the loss of his wife, his spirit was broken. The death of the princess was not only a vast psychological loss for him, but also an enormous practical deficit. Since she was a tremendous shamanic professional that could foresee and manipulate supernatural forces, losing her created a desperate and devastating situation for him and his troops. Kojiki and Nihonshoki illustrate the loss of Ototachibanahime as the beginning of the end for the great hero. He still possessed great power and extraordinary military prowess, but was not as invincible as the time when he had a great assistant. Since no one in his troops could foresee the spiritual forces behind

---

85   Wikipedia: Brahmin. Online at http://en.wikipedia.org/wiki/Brahmin

the enemies, he was more vulnerable in wars. This incident led his luck and military career to decline gradually and eventually bring his life to an end.

After losing Ototachibanahime, Takeru married another woman Miyazuhime[86] in Owari district before returning to Yamato. After marrying her, he left Kusanagi the holy sword and continued to travel to the capital of Yamato. His divine powers were coming from the family treasures from Susa-no-Ō. The legend does not state the reason he left the sword behind. Now, his supernatural force was in grave danger.

He then encountered another misfortune and that was to lose Takeinadane[87] one of his most trusted subordinates. He died suddenly, and neither Kojiki nor Nihonshoki state the details or exact cause of his death. However, the direct cause of death was most likely either heart attack or stroke, since he didn't have any illness.

Yamato Takeru eventually became more vulnerable, started losing in battlefields and eventually received a mortal wound in Mount Ibuki (伊吹山)[88] which led him to death. Mount Ibuki is known as a spiritual mountain throughout the whole history of Japan, and there is a belief that a powerful Kami resides there. The deity of the mountain took a form of a gigantic serpent and blocked the way of the troops of Takeru heading back to the province of Yamato after a long journey to conquer the Ezo. According to the legend, Takeru received a serious injury when he took up his sword and tried to kill him,

---

86   Wikipedia: 宮簀媛. Online at http://ja.wikipedia.org/wiki/%E5%AE%AE%E7%B0%80%E5%AA%9B

87   Wikipedia: 建稲種命. Online at http://ja.wikipedia.org/wiki/%E5%BB%BA%E7%A8%B2%E7%A8%AE%E5%91%BD

88   Wikipedia: 伊吹山. Online at http://ja.wikipedia.org/wiki/%E4%BC%8A%E5%90%B9%E5%B1%B1

since the serpent was more powerful than he thought. Besides that, Takeru became mortally ill after the injury. However, the legend does not state why he became ill and what kind of illness he had, and the direct cause of his death remains in mystery.

The legend simply stated that Takeru was defeated by a powerful deity of the mountain. However, Kazuha Ogura (1989)[89] maintains that he could be involved in a conflict between mountain tribes of this district by being asked to assist one of them. It could be a trouble about mines of iron, since Mount Ibuki was rich in iron and other minerals, and a serpent is almost always a symbol of iron in Japanese mythology. The legend also stated that soldiers had to carry Takeru to the land of Nobono (能褒野) in Ise (伊勢) Province, since he had a serious illness besides the injury. Ogura also stated that the Mount Ibuki is rich in herbal plants, including toxic spices as well as minerals, and speculated that he could have received an arrow with poison made of the local plants.

After the hero is severely wounded in Mount Ibuki and becomes mortally ill, his soldiers carry him to the land of Nobono in Ise Province not far from the capital of Yamato for local physicians to treat him. They were close to home, the capital of the nation from which they came. However, his illness proved serious that no physician could rescue him. I have to agree with Ogura's hypotheses that his fatal illness was caused by an arrow with some toxic substance for there to be any historical fact behind the legend. If he had a serious enough injury at war, he would have died immediately from blood loss. Instead, he died from an illness he contracted after the battle.

89   Kazuha Ogura, Amakakeru Shiratori Yamato Takeru [Yamato Takeru, a swan running in the sky]. (Tokyo: Kawadeshobo, 1989)

Any wound in a battle before the Seventh Century would not cause such an illness that no physicians could treat, unless it was accompanied by a toxic substance.

With his last breath, the hero expresses appreciation to his soldiers. His last glance went to his men and the majestic mountains around him. Upon his death, the prince expresses how beautiful the land of Yamato and mountains are[90].

When Yamato Takeru died in the land of Nobono, his soul transforms into a great white swan and flies away to the sky after visiting various parts of the country, particularly the Yamato region. The writers of Kojiki and Nihonshoki are ingenious in their description that the hero transforms into a bird as it follows neither Shinto nor Buddhism concepts of the afterlife. Perhaps, they have compiled the whole knowledge newly obtained from literatures, mythologies and philosophies from China and incorporated it to the story of Yamato Takeru. Knowledge from China does not necessarily mean that it is originated in China. It may have originated in India, Middle East, Greece or Europe and travelled through the Silk Road to China. The Silk Road was the main artery of the ancient world that played a vital role to transport, people, animals, goods and knowledge from the east to the west or vice versa. Nevertheless, Japanese intellectuals in the Seventh Century fervently studied Chinese writings, because China was the only accessible place for their global knowledge.

From the time of antiquity, birds have been symbols of power and freedom[91]. Toshihiko Moriya (1968)[92] maintains

---

90   Ogura. ibid.
91   The CBS International Business Network: Birds in Mythology, 2011. Online at http://findarticles.com/p/articles/mi_gx5219/is_2000/ai_n19133797/
92   Moriya. Ibid.

that birds were considered as symbols of human souls. In many ancient cultures, they were considered as travelers coming from the afterlife or creatures that could travel through different realms of the universe because of their ability to fly. They also believed some birds were souls without bodies able to fly and travel to a different world.

Many myths around the world have also linked birds to the arrival or departure to the world of the living[93]. For instance, in some cultures, including the West, they have been associated with birth, claiming that a person's soul arrived on earth in the avian form. In the Western world, there is a traditional answer to a child's question "Where do babies come from?" The answer is "The stork brings them". Many ancient myths and legends have also linked birds to the journeys undertaken by human souls after death. According to an article, *Birds in Mythology* from *Mythencyclopedia.com*[94], many myths and legends around the world, link birds with the forms that the souls of the dead take during the travel to the afterworld. The article stated that:

> The Greeks and Celts thought that the dead could reappear as birds. The Sumerians of the ancient Near East believed that the dead existed as birds in the underworld. According to Islamic tradition, all dead souls remain in the form of birds until Judgment Day, while in Christian tradition, the gentle dove became a symbol of the immortal soul ascending to heaven. Birds also appear in Hindu mythology as symbols of the soul or as forms taken by the soul between earthly lives. The connection between birds and souls is sometimes reflected in

93   The CBS International Business Network: Birds in Mythology, 2011. Online at http://findarticles.com/p/articles/mi_gx5219/is_2000/ai_n19133797/
94   Birds in Mythology: Mythencyclopedia.com, 2011. Online at http://findarticles.com/p/articles/mi_gx5219/is_2000/ai_n19133797/

language. A Turkish saying describes somebody's death as "His soul bird has flown away (2011).

In most ancient cultures, birds were considered forms that the dead are going to take as he or she travels to the afterlife. However, in Christian tradition, the dove is not a posthumous form of the dead, but it symbolizes the Holy Spirit, the third person of the Godhead or the substantial essence or nature of one and only God. Humans must remain in the same forms even after the death, since they are only creatures created in the image of God. This is another way that makes Christianity unique and distinct from all other belief systems around the world in the ancient and modern days.

However, Christians may share the same mentality to fly away from the earth after death as those who lived in many different parts of the world during the mythological ages. There is a Christian hymn titled *I'll Fly Away*[95] written by Albert E. Brumley in 1929 that expresses the idea that Christians will also fly away from the earth after the end of their lives. This belief does not contradict the teaching of the Bible because it also teaches that all believers are going to the heaven. However, this does not mean one takes on avian forms either in heaven or during the journey to get there.

Besides these, the ancient Egyptians believed the soul of the dead could leave the body in an avian form, usually a hawk. Therefore, they built their tombs and graves with narrow passages leading to the open air so that these birds could fly in and out. In general a bird symbolizes the soul of the dead, but sometimes it acts as a guide in the afterworld. For instance, in

---

95   Wikipedia: I'll Fly Away. Online at http://en.wikipedia.org/wiki/I%27ll_Fly_Away

Syrian tradition, icons of eagles on tombs represent the guides who lead souls to the afterlife.

Probably, the writers of these two narratives were exposed to the myths, legends and poems about birds from Africa, Middle East and many other parts of the world through Chinese documents that traveled via the Silk Road. The intelligentsia with Chinese education must have been greatly inspired by the new knowledge from around the world, although they were not able to travel and visit many locations of this planet the way that birds can. At the same time, these individuals might have a fantasy of becoming birds themselves and flying over the horizon sometime after the end of their earthly life.

Kojiki and Nihonshoki also have several differences regarding the stories that the great swan, Yamato Takeru, said his last farewell to loved ones in an avian form. In Nihonshoki, he encountered his father Emperor Keikō, who lost his appetite following the loss of his son. After the burial of the prince the emperor saw a swan coming out of the tomb and flying to the direction of Yamato. Later, as he and his soldiers open the tomb and looked inside, he discovers nothing except the clothes of the dead prince.

On the other hand, according to Kojiki there is no such description that the emperor deeply grieved or saw a swan flying out of the tomb in keeping with his consistent descriptions that Takeru was in a conflicting relationship with his father. In Kojiki, the swan greets his wives and children who survive him, but his father is excluded. Then, they followed after the bird reading poems to lament his death. This honest and unflattering description about the monarchy might indicate that the first chronicle was more loyal to the original story of Yamato Takeru passed throughout centuries through the method of the oral transmission during the illiterate ages.

But the story of the second chronicle that Emperor Keikō met the swan flying out of the tomb carries an artificial tone. The second narrative also conveys an impression that it was written by those who simply followed the policy of the government. Alternatively, they could be imperial loyalists that had idealized the royal family and firmly believe that all emperors of Japan had perfect and flawless god-like characters.

Nevertheless, these discourses in the ancient chronicles in which Yamato Takeru became a swan and greeted those who survived him, were ingenious and creative. It seems that these stories from the Seventh Century most likely stemmed from the same source material that originated in the Middle East or North Africa. The original ideas were likely transported to China across the Silk Road a long time before Japanese scholars studied them.

The difference between the qualities of the two chronicles as literary arts lie in the level of freedom that writers had when they were engaged in their projects. The writers of Kojiki integrated a foreign idea that the dead hero transformed into a bird with a traditional story coming from the either Yayoi or Kofun Period the previous era through oral transmission. They were enterprising to adopt a new concept from a foreign land while being loyal to their own tradition. Therefore, their literature bloomed as one of the most beautiful literary arts in the ancient world. The writers of Nihonshoki were also progressive and innovative in a sense, but unfortunately failed to liberate their fancies and imagination in their work, since they were forced to produce the document under strict control of the government. Therefore, the quality of the second chronicle as literature falls short of the standard of literary arts in antiquity and is not comparable to the first one.

Yamato Takeru & King Arthur

C. Scott Littleton maintains that there are quite a few similarities between the legend of Yamato Takeru and the British King Arthur[96] legend[97]. According to him, the storylines and main motifs between the two stories are amazingly similar. Littleton states that:

> Of all the heroes in Japanese legendry, none is more "Arthurian" than Yamato-takeru, "The Brave of Yamato." Indeed, the tales of Yamato-takeru's strength, courage, leadership, feats of arms, love affairs, magical sword, and untimely death all bear a remarkable resemblance to the legends surrounding the life and death of King Arthur, as related in Sir Thomas Malory's Le Morte D'Arthur and a host of other medieval British and continental texts. In the present paper I propose that the legends of these two heroes, as well as those of Lancelot du Lac and Batraz (a hero celebrated by the Ossetians of the north-central Caucasus), all derive from the same ancient source, and that this heroic tradition has managed to span the Eurasian landmass from one end to the other. But before proceeding to this comparison, let us summarize the relevant portions of the legend of Yamato-takeru (1995).

For instance, both Arthur and Yamato Takeru receive magical, divine swords from powerful and mysterious female characters that endow them with invincible superhuman aptitude. These swords are closely associated with the extraordinary power and invincible military prowess of the

---

96   Wikipedia: King Arthur. Online at http://en.wikipedia.org/wiki/King_Arthur
97   C. Scott Littleton. Yamato-takeru: An "Arthurian" Hero in Japanese Tradition. Asian Folklore Studies, Volume 54, 1995. 259-274

heroes. Takeru obtains *Kusanagi* from Yamatohime, his aunt and a powerful priestess, while Arthur receives the second *Excalibur*, from the *Lady of the Lake*. Both heroes lose their power and receive a mortal wound or illness which leads them to death after they gave up the swords. They eventually collapse during a conflict with a powerful adversary and die after giving up the magical sword to a female figure. Takeru leaves the sword to Miyazuhime and Arthur to the Lady of the Lake. At the end of the stories, both heroes are transported to the afterworld, one in the form of a swan and the other on a barge. Because of these intriguing similarities, Littleton entitles Yamato Takeru an "Arthurian" hero. He drew a conclusion that the two legends share the same source from the Ancient Near East.

Littleton maintains that the story of Lancelot,[98] one of one of the Knights of the Round Table and Arthur's most trusted sidekick, and Batraz,[99] an Iranian hero, also have similar characteristics. He concludes that Yamato Takeru, Arthur, Lancelot and Batraz all appear to derive from a common Northeast Iranian heroic, and perhaps ultimately divine, prototype.

This supports the story that the hero's soul transformation into a swan probably originated in the myths, legends and poems about birds from Africa, Middle East came from China. King Arthur was transported into the afterworld on a barge without transforming into an avian, likely because the writers of the Arthurian legend did not have access to the same materials about the soul becoming a bird.

---

98   Wikipedia: Lancelot. Online at http://en.wikipedia.org/wiki/Lancelot
99   Wikipedia: Batraz. Online at http://en.wikipedia.org/wiki/Batraz

Nevertheless, it seems possible the writers of these two documents used the same materials from Northern Iran regarding the character of a divine sword, the way that the heroes received it and the mortal wound or illness suffered after giving it away. Hieda no Are and other writers of Kojiki and Nihonshoki seemed to have access to the story of Batraz transported to China from the Middle East across the Silk Road. Thus, at the end of his article Littleton[100] makes a concluding remark that:

> In sum, I suggest that both Japanese and European legendry were subject to Northeast Iranian cultural influences at approximately the same period of time (from the second to the fifth centuries A.D.), and that this is why the legends of Yamato-takeru have such an Arthurian feel to them (1995).

Before the Seventh Century, however, Japan was an illiterate society, people lived savage, extremely primitive lifestyle. No one there was capable of study foreign documents and integrates ideas from them into their own legends, or even to produce a single written document. Therefore it does not seem likely that Japanese legendry was subject to Northeast Iranian cultural influences from the Second to the Fifth centuries A.D. as Littleton states. At around the end of the Seventh Century Japan made a dramatic transition from a mere collection of savage tribes into a civilized nation-state with a centralized government. The leaders during this era were extremely eager to acquire literacy and knowledge from China, since it was one of only a few nations with literacy and advanced civilization and possessed highly developed technology and a state-governing system based on Taoism,

---

100   Littleton. ibid.

Confucianism and Buddhism. The Japanese emperor's court drove almost all literate intelligentsia who had attained Chinese education, to complete Kojiki and Nihonshoki, the most archaic written narratives of the nation[101]. Those who were engaged in the compilation of these two documents were well versed in the knowledge coming from all over including the Northeast Iranian legend.

---

101   Ebihara. Shinto War Gods of Yasukuni Shrine. ibid.

[102] Yamato Takeru no Mikoto. Taiso, Yoshitoshi (1839-1892)[103].

---

102   Bookmark This Record: http://www.loc.gov/pictures/item/2009615033/.
103   The picture is used under "fair dealing" (Canada) and "fair use" (USA) provisions in copyright law.

2

Spirituality & Afterlife Concept in Medieval Japan

The belief systems among the Japanese population during the Middle Ages were much more complicated than the previous ages, since Buddhism, Taoism and many other schools of the spirituality were already introduced from China and Korean peninsula and settled in the archipelago.

The era of Asuka Period (飛鳥時代: 592-645)[104] followed the Kofun Period. After this came the Heian Period (平安時代: 794 to 1185)[105] and Kamakura Period (鎌倉時代: 1185-1333)[106]. Various belief systems stemmed from a mixed tradition of Shinto, Buddhism, Taoism and others that came into existence and thrived.

Ghost stories from the *Tales of Ise* (伊勢物語)[107] and the *Tale of the Heike* (平家物語)[108] written in the Eighth and Twelfth centuries contain a rich variety and depth of the spiritual beliefs among the medieval Japanese.

---

104   Wikipedia: Asuka period. Online at http://en.wikipedia.org/wiki/Asuka_period
105   Wikipedia: Heian period. Online at http://en.wikipedia.org/wiki/Heian_period
106   Wikipedia: Kamakura period. Online at http://en.wikipedia.org/wiki/Kamakura_period
107   Wikipedia: The Tales of Ise. Online at http://en.wikipedia.org/wiki/The_Tales_of_Ise
108   Wikipedia: The Tale of the Heike. Online at http://en.wikipedia.org/wiki/The_Tale_of_the_Heike

Early Development of Japanese Buddhism

Great arts and new technologies that migrated from the continent characterized the Asuka Period, and magnificent architectural structures and Buddhist sculptures that were created in this era still remain today. After Japan acquired the state-governing system, a more developed technology, literacy and knowledge from China, their belief system about the spiritual world and afterlife increased in complexities and sophistication. During this Period, many significant artistic, social, and political transformations took place in Japan, and people there developed new belief systems based on Buddhism. However, they did not totally abandon the old Shinto based animistic belief, but synthesized it with new thought. The synchronization of two different belief systems made Japan a society with the dual faith of Shinto and Buddhism. After this, the two faiths coexisted in a very unique way for more than a millennium.

One example of the early development of Buddhist monasteries in Mount Miwa has been studied by Anna Andreeva, (三輪山)[109] the Yamato which was once a center of Kami worship of Shinto. She contends that archaeological, mythological, and literary evidence attests to the importance of Mount Miwa as a powerful ritual center in prehistoric times[110]. She maintains that both Kojiki and Nihonshoki contain numerous records concerning a ritual site at the foot of Mount Miwa.

Mount Miwa was an extinct volcano located in the south-eastern corner of the Yamato province and considered a divine

---

109   Wikipedia: 三輪山. Online at http://ja.wikipedia.org/wiki/%E4%B8%89%E8%BC%AA%E5%B1%B1

110   Andreeva. ibid.

mountain since the Jomon Period and a centre of Proto-Shinto ritual practices. If the theory of Minoru Haiyama[111] is correct, the cannibalism and human sacrifice was performed as sacred Shinto rituals in the cultic site of this mountain. The memory of the prehistoric practice of human sacrifice was suppressed and thrown into oblivion during the Asuka Period when government leaders tried to exhibit the sign of civilization and discard barbarism inherited from the previous era. The human sacrifice stayed dormant until State Shinto in the 20th century revived a form of sacrifice, though without the cannibalism, during the Second World War. This came in the form of the special attack corps well known as *Kamikaze Party*[112] that carried out suicide attacks[113]. Ironically, State Shinto followed the custom of the matriarchical Jomon society that sacrificed only males. They also deified the dead soldiers who crashed their planes into American aircraft carriers, just as those in Jomon period did for the sacrificed men, Kami.

Buddhist monasteries developed in Mount Miwa after the introduction of a new belief system sometime during Asuka Period, although the exact time was unknown. Andreeva observes that the two belief systems influenced each other over centuries, and produced esoteric and mysterious tantric practices in the same mountain region. Since the government after the Asuka Period sponsored the integration of Shinto and Buddhism, the sacred site at Mount Miwa developed into a unique complex with a dual function as a Shinto shrine and Buddhist temple. She states that the forms of tantric practice of Shinto developed at the Ōmiwa shrine-temple multiplex was

---

111   Haiyama, ibid
112   *Kamikaze*: 神風 meant "wind of Kami or god."
113   Ebihara. Shinto War Gods of Yasukuni Shrine. ibid.

influenced to a great extent by the ritualism and doctrine of
Esoteric Buddhism[114].

Andreeva also maintains that the serpent deity
Ōmononushi (大物主), the "Great Spirit Master," the chief
deity of Mount Miwa, played an important role in Shinto-
Buddhism synchronization. Ōmononushi is an indigenous deity
who appears in a story of a divine marriage to a daughter
of a local chieftain, and as a deity causing a great plague.
The legend states that the snake god was pacified when he
received the chieftain's daughter as his bride. Since the theme
of pacification was an important theme for Buddhists, they
also tried to pacify this powerful deity by their own method[115].
According to Andreeva:

> An important motivation for the Buddhist pacification
> of Miwa could be the Miwa deity itself. Its origins as the
> serpent deity Ōmononushi were known from the old
> legends, which described a divine union between the
> snake god of Miwa and the daughter of a local chieftain.
> In the Buddhist view, kami, particularly those of a "real
> kind"(実者) who manifested themselves as snakes, were
> perceived as "cursing kami" (tatarigami祟神) and beings
> who were at the origin of the eight sins, or delusions.

The term Satori (悟り) or "enlightenment," which means
'freedom from the darkness', is currently a magical spell for
Buddhists to convert evil people or deities into good ones.
According to this belief, the Miwa deity is an "unruly deity" and
a kami of ignorance who had not yet made even the first step
towards enlightenment. Andreeva notes that such kami had
outstanding capacities and could potentially serve as a source

---

114   Andreeva. ibid.
115   Andreeva. ibid.

of enlightenment, but they also needed to be subjugated and brought into the Buddhist realm.

According to this logic, the Buddhists could bring even Lucifer[116] into the state of enlightenment and make him a good and benevolent deity, or restore him into the Angel of Light. The philosophical assumption of this thinking is based on humanism that entrusts the inerrant goodness of mankind and the will power to get better. This has a close parallel to the philosophy of *Enlightenment* that was prevalent between 18th to 20th centuries in the West. The Enlightenment philosophy placed confidence in the human intellect and reasoning ability. In other words, the Enlightenment philosophy was a symbol of modernism that made men feel so potent and proud that they started thinking of themselves as God[117]. The philosphies of the Enlightenment philosophy could be said to have contributed to the acceptance of Western colonialism and attitudes to nuclear arms and the environment.

Andreeva also maintains that the Sun goddess *Amaterasu* also mutated into a Buddhist deity in the 'scientific lab' of these ambitious monks in the ancient capital of Japan. She introduces a Buddhist document entitled Miwa daimyōjin engi, arguing that Amaterasu the Sun goddess and the progenitor of the imperial family evolved into a very significant Buddhist deity. She quotes that:

> The Miwa daimyōjin engi relates a number of theories, some of which could be of local origin. On the other hand, some theories appearing in this text contain many threads of esoteric and mythological knowledge that could be traced back to the esoteric Buddhist circles at Ise. For instance, the engi cites an oracle according to which the

116   Wikipedia: Lucifer. Online at http://en.wikipedia.org/wiki/Lucifer
117   Ebihara. Shinto War Gods of Yasukuni Shrine. ibid.

august name of Amaterasu or Tenshō Kōtaijin, translates as the sacred name of Buddha Mahāvairocana of Two Realms, the "All-Illuminating Bright Wisdom and the King of Heavenly Golden Wheel, Dainichi" 天金輪王光明遍照大日尊 . According to that theory, Amaterasu is a manifestation of Mahāvairocana's Three Bodies in One 三身即一之大日, which is the "original ground" (honji本地) of the imperial ancestor.

The term *engi* (縁起) has several different meanings, but in this context refers to origin or upbringing. The document explains the origin of a Buddhist deity named *Miwa daimyōjin* and draws a conclusion that she was formally Sun goddess Amaterasu who is the imperial ancestor. Andreeva continues her argument that the sacred document further explains that Dainichi, formerly Amaterasu, appears to the universe in its Corresponding Body, Reward Body and Dharma Body, in effect, citing the Mahāvairocana Sūtra, one of the essential scriptures of Esoteric Buddhism[118].

Later, Amaterasu also establishes her new position in the Japanese Lotus Sutra (妙法蓮華経) modified by Nichiren (日蓮)[119] a Buddhist monk who lived during the Kamakura Period (1185–1333). He renamed Amaterasu into *Tenshozenjin* (天照善神) and counted her as one of the good heavenly deities. Nichiren was well known as an anti-establishment leader in 12th century Japan who encountered persecutions and imprisonment. His teaching became very popular among the lower classes, or under-privileged population, and is still influential in today's Japanese society.

After the introduction of Buddhism in the Asuka Period, the Japanese developed various afterlife concepts during the

---

118   Andreeva. ibid.
119   Wikipedia: Nichiren. Online at http://en.wikipedia.org/wiki/Nichiren

medieval era. Previously, they simply believed in the entrance to land of Yomi, or becoming Kami if they made exceptional achievements during their life time. The new afterlife objectives include a better life next time, the reincarnation in the Pure Land, becoming a Bodhisattva, or a Buddhist deity after death.

Self-immolation

Brian Ruppert (2008) maintains that the custom of self-immolation[120], or the act of setting fire to oneself, which aimed at post-mortem transformation into Bodhisattva was introduced to the archipelago during the medieval age[121]. This custom, according to Ruppert, stemmed from the numerous tales of the early lives of Siddhārtha Gautama, (563 BCE - 483 BCE)[122] the historical Buddha, in which he accumulated his merits by giving up his body through self-sacrifice at the end of each life. Inspired by early narratives from Indian, Chinese and Japanese Buddhists came not only legends of bodhisattvas' self-sacrifice, but also the practice of self-mutilation and suicide. Ruppert also introduces a story of an anonymous monk of Satsuma province who made a tremendous effort to purify himself and pursued self-mortification. He states that:

> His efforts culminate in his self-immolation, which the narrative describes as no different from that of the bodhisattva beheld with Joy by All Living Beings, described in the Lotus Sutra and discussed above, who immolated himself in the presence of a Buddha-relic stupa. Indeed, three days after the monk's self sacrifice, his disciples find a large quantity of Buddha relics, indicating the monk's piety and mysterious association with the

120   Wikipedia: Self-immolation. Online at http://en.wikipedia.org/wiki/Self-immolation
121   Brian Ruppert. Beyond Death & Afterlife. Death & the Afterlife in Japanese Buddhism (Honolulu, HI: USA. University of Hawai Press, 2008) 102-136
122   Wikipedia: Gautama Buddha. Online at http://en.wikipedia.org/wiki/Gautama_Buddha

bodhisattva while at the same time illustrating the thematic association of self-sacrifice with the worship and acquisition of relics.

Ruppert concludes his statement that the tale draws together relics and Pure Land practice, perhaps suggesting that actions evoking the line of argument concerning relics also contribute to attaining birth in Amida's realm[123]. These monks endured the whole process, and pursued rebirth as bodhisattvas in the Pure Land since it was an ultimate practice of the Lotus Sutra according to their belief. They did it so as to realize their great dream and ambition to save billions of souls of humans and other sentient beings after successfully transforming into powerful deities in the Buddhist world.

According to Mark L. Blum (2008), the custom of self-mortification or ritual suicide stemmed from three sources. The first factor comes from Indian Buddhist doctrinal traditions regarding self-mutilation and suicide. The second factor comes from Chinese and later Japanese monastic traditions validating suicide as a successful rebirth such as bodhisattvas. They practiced it following the Pure Land Buddhism tradition in China and Japan for the purpose of attaining birth in the Pure Land. The third factor is a traditional view of martyrdom in medieval China and Japan based on a Confucian value, and in Japan's case, also incorporating ancient cultural patterns of corporate identity mixed with medieval traditions of warrior suicide[124].

Blum also maintains that there was a time in which the imperial court prohibited ritual suicide, sometime around the

123   Ruppert. ibid.
124   Mark L. Blum. Collective Suicide at the Funeral of Jitsunyo. Death & the Afterlife in Japanese Buddhism (Honolulu, HI: USA. University of Hawai Press, 2008) 137-174

Seventh Century. They banned the custom because the court official was afraid that the ritual suicide of certain individuals might develop into political martyrdom to promote rebellion against the government. For instance, there were several women who committed suicide after the death of a husband or brother who had been put to death due to a political crime. Nevertheless, the custom of ritual suicide became more and more popular and fashionable, and no government authority could stop it. Blum also contends that in the latter half of the Heian Period, there was a trend to follow a certain strict procedure of the ritual for a guarantee of rebirth in the Pure Land[125] as he states:

> Especially in the latter half of the period, references to suicide in an explicitly Buddhist context increases, and those associated with aspiration for birth in Amida's Pure Land emerge as the most numerous of all. This link between suicide and Pure Land belief and practice may be seen as one aspect of a broader gestalt whereby motivation for self-destruction is grounded in the belief that ritual suicide done properly could propel one to afterlife in one of the paradisiacal pure lands associated, not only with Amida, but also with the bodhisattvas Miroku (Skt. Maitreya) and Kannon (Avalokitesvara).

According to Blum, *Kannon* (観音)[126] and *Miroku,* (弥勒)[127] there were other popular Buddhist deities besides Amida during the Heian Period. Both Miroku or Maitreya, and Kannon were originally disciples of the historical Śākyamuni Buddha and later, enlightened, became bodhisattvas, according to Buddhist legend.

---

125   Blum. ibid.
126   Kwannon: Encyclo Online Encyclopedia, 2011. Online at http://www.encyclo. co.uk/define/kwannon
127   Wikipedia: 弥勒菩薩. Online at http://ja.wikipedia.org/wiki/%E5%BC%A5%E5% 8B%92%E8%8F%A9%E8%96%A9

Kannon was originally a male, *Avalokiteśvara,* who lived in India. He went through training under Gautama Siddhārtha until he achieved enlightenment. Contrary to this historical account, Kannon is generally considered as a female deity, which embodies the compassion and mercy of all bodhisattvas among Japanese Buddhists. On the other hand, some Buddhists believe that all bodhisattvas are gender neutral, so that Kannon is neither male nor female.

Miroku was also a male and disciple of Gautama Buddha in India and named M*aitreya.* According to legend, he was appointed to be a future Buddha by Siddhārtha or the historical Buddha. According to this belief, he is currently in a place called *Tosotsuten* (兜率天)[128] or *Tusita* and going through training to attain the 'Buddha-hood,' the highest rank among the Buddhist deities such as a bodhisattva and a rank lower than the Buddha. They also believe that he is coming out of the Tusita in 5,760 million years after his earthly life as a Buddha to complete the salvation of all sentient life forms, since his training is to be completed by then.

As the belief systems became more complex and diverse, the suicide rituals which aimed at the rebirth in the Pure Land also developed complexity, diversity and in specifications. However, the measurement of their effectiveness was completely subjective, since there was no way of testing the hypotheses.

Cremation

Brian Ruppert maintained that the concept of self-sacrifice coming from India also produced a custom of

---

128   **Wikipedia:** 兜率天. **Online at** http://ja.wikipedia.org/wiki/%E5%85%9C%E7%8E%87%E5%A4%A9

cremation at funerals[129]. He states that medieval Japanese monks read a sutra in which an Indian bodhisattva wrapped himself in jewels and burned his body in an offering to the Buddha in the Pure Land, the self-immolation. This teaching was later interpreted in a milder way and produced the custom of cremation after death that is prevalent in the Japanese society even today. Japanese Buddhists started believing that not only conduct during one's life time, but also the way funerals are performed affects the karma, or the well being, in the next life. Since then, the general public also believed that the dead could accumulate their merits if his or her body was consumed by fire and broken into pieces. Ruppert states:

> Here, the Buddha, who is described as being eternal and void in his person, is said to have left his bones out of compassion for sentient beings. That is, he allows his indestructible body to be broken into pieces in order that beings may plane "good roots" (zenkon) through the act of venerating them — this in spite of the temporal distance from the smoke rising out of Śākyamuni's[130] ashes.

According to the legend, the body of Śākyamuni or Siddhārtha, the historical Gautama Buddha reached Parinirvana, or the final deathless state upon his death. His remains were cremated and his ashes turned into Śarīra or relics like shiny beads. Legend also states that the Śarīra[131] was spread around all over the world as precious and magical substance sometime after the reign of King Ashoka (304–232 BC)[132] and stored in pagodas in Buddhist temples. Japanese called Śarīra busshari (仏舎利) and lengends states it was

---

129   Ruppert. ibid.
130   Śākyamuni is another name of Siddhārtha or Gautama Buddha.
131   Wikipedia: Śarīra. Online at http://en.wikipedia.org/wiki/Sarira
132   Wikipedia: Ashoka. Online at http://en.wikipedia.org/wiki/Ashoka_the_Great

preserved it in their historical pagodas in Nara and Kyoto as well.

Custom of Self-Mummification

The custom of self-immolation often took a form of mummification during the medieval era. Many Japanese Buddhist monks voluntarily went through the process to terminate themselves to preserve their remains as mummies. They did it so since they were greatly inspired to become bodhisattvas in the Pure Land after completing the process.

Catrien Ross (1996) who has lived in Japan from the late 20th century and practices Energy Medicine, studied the process of self-mummification of the monks of Mount Gassan (月山) in Yamagata Prefecture[133]. She describes it as follows:

> The most rigours of practices, however, was undertaken by the "living mummies" of Gassan, who had to remain celibate and give up eating meat and also eventually rice, wheat, and other grains. For a time, they subsisted only on mountain vegetables and fruits and nuts, with the quantities of food gradually growing smaller until the amounts dwindled to amount nothing. The body, too, shrank and dried out, and the monk would over time turn into a stringy "living mummy," who, thus transformed, would die in his chosen holy spot.

They were confined in very a small room with an extremely low ceiling when they died. The ceiling was connected to the surface by a bamboo pipe, so that air could come, and they could breathe until the very moment they died. When these priests died, the fellow monks opened the tomb and examined if the bodies were fully mummified. Only few were fully mummified and successfully raised to the rank of bodhisattva.

---

133   Catrien Ross. Japanese Ghost Stories. (North Clarendon, VT: USA: Tuttle Publishing, 1996)

Before sealing the mummies back into their tombs, they removed all internal organs and brains from the remains in order to prevent future decay and corruption.

The mummy as the end product of the entire procedure is also called *sokushinbutsu* (即身仏)[134] or the bodhisattva in a body. It carries an idea that both soul and body of the priest become bodhisattvas and achieve the status of enlightenment in the process of mummification. About 24 bodies of self-mummified Buddhist monks still remain in various parts of Japan today.

Ross also maintains that according to the local Buddhist belief around Mount Gassan, many monks who failed the process of self-mummification often became wondering ghosts and haunted the temples. She notes that a local priest reported he had seen several ghosts around his temple, including those who died without completing the mummy training successfully. According to his report, he found a ghost on the roof, another in the cherry tree, and one more in white standing before a tomb[135]. It seems the practice of self-mummification was an exam to become bodhisattva and that these priests had only one this chance in their present life for the rest of eternity.

Appeasement of Vengeful Spirits

Takeshi Umehara (b.1925)[136] maintains that Buddhist sutra and chanting were often used as tools of appeasement of vengeful spirits[137]. Umehara (1974) argues that Japanese

---

134   Wikipedia: ミイラ. Online at http://ja.wikipedia.org/wiki/%E5%8D%B3%E8%BA%AB%E4%BB%8F#.E5.8D.B3.E8.BA.AB.E4.BB.8F

135   Ross. ibid.

136   Wikipedia: 梅原猛. Online at http://ja.wikipedia.org/wiki/%E6%A2%85%E5%8E%9F%E7%8C%9B

137   Takeshi Umehara. The Genealogy of Avenging Spirits. Sage, 1974

culture is profoundly influenced by the concept of avenging spirits. According to his definition, they are souls possessed by resentment or the desire for revenge. They are unable to find a resting place and wander around eternally, since they experience painful death caused by a betrayal, treason or profound sorrow. Umehara maintains that the fear of spirits of the dead was once prevalent all over the world. However, according to him, in Europe and China, under the influence of Christianity or of Confucianism, this kind of fear diminishes or disappears at an early date. According to Christian doctrine, the dead are not able to stay in the realm of the living and curse anyone since he or she goes to heaven or hell at the end of earthly life. The Japanese also acquired Confucianism from China, yet unlike the Chinese, they did not believe that this teaching was strong enough to annihilate the cursing power of vengeful spirits.

Umehara's study indicates that avenging spirits are found in the Genji-Monogatari (源氏物語), the *Tale of Genji*,[138] a novel written by Lady *Murasaki Shikibu*[139], which Umehara admires as a historical landmark. The vengeful spirits which required the appeasement in her novel belong to the women victimized by the promiscuous lifestyle of Prince Genji, the protagonist, and a semi-historical person in 11th century Japan. He was a frivolous aristocrat who had no control of his sexual impulse and slept with many women in the imperial court. Genji's extremely sensual and irresponsible lifestyle that victimized numerous women in the court was a notable imperial scandal that caught the attention of the author.

138   Wikipedia: The Tale of Genji. Online at http://en.wikipedia.org/wiki/The_Tale_of_ Genji
139   Wikipedia: Murasaki Shikibu. Online at http://en.wikipedia.org/wiki/Murasaki_ Shikibu

In Genji-Monogatari, Murasaki Shikibu eloquently illustrates a series of vengeances performed by the spirits, first by the living, and then by the dead Rokujo-Myasudokoro, Prince Genji's lover who eliminates all her rivals. Umehara contends that during the time of Prince Genji, people believed in the cursing power of both living and dead people, so that they used both Shinto and Buddhist rituals to eliminate the curse. According to the belief system during this era, spirits of the dead were considered extremely powerful, giving rise to the theory that the leitmotif of the novel is the concept of vengeance. Toward the end of the story, the souls of these women victimized by the actions of Prince Genji who suffer painful deaths, finally find resting places and comfort by receiving the appeasement based on the Buddhist teaching. Those who were still living found peace in their minds by making a decision to forgive the perpetrator. Among scholars of Japanese literature there is a consensus that Lady Murasaki must be a devout Buddhist, although she is a mystery woman whose exact identity remains unknown.

Appeasement of Significant People in History

According to Umehara, Japanese performed religious rites to pacify angry spirits long before the introduction of Buddhism. However, Buddhism has become established in Japan, mainly because it fulfilled the role of peace-maker more effectively than had the Japanese rites of worshipping the gods since ancient times[140].

The appeasement of ghosts or dead subjects in medieval Japan has a wide variety. They were generally those who suffered a painful or tragic death with a vengeful thought

---

140   Umehara. ibid.

against the perpetrators or all of humanity. They include monks who fail the process of self-mummification and become wondering ghosts who haunted the temple, as well as others who failed in different types of self-immolation. According to various legends, human ghosts often transformed into Yōkai (妖怪)[141] and Oni (鬼)[142], preternatural creatures in the Japanese folklore and mythological world when they experienced some sort of extreme emotional state such as extraordinary grief, intense jealousy, rage, wrath, pain or vengeful thoughts upon their death. They have lost humanity and transformed into vampire like creatures because they cursed the world and humanity.

Furthermore, several prominent individuals in real Japanese history were also considered to possess vengeful spirits, which required appeasement, according to Umehara. They include *Shotoku Taishi* (574-622)[143], Sugawara-no-Michizane (845 - 903)[144], Taïra-no-Masakado (平将門: died 940)[145], Minamoto-no-Yoshitsune (1159 – 1189)[146] and the forty-seven Samurai (四十七士) of Ako[147], who had been put to death during the Edo Period (江戸時代: 1603 – 1868)[148] in the early modern era. These individuals were well known by the general public in Japan and played important roles in Japanese history. They were also highly respected heroes by many in the

141   Wikipedia: Yōkai. ibid
142   Wikipedia: Oni (folklore). ibid.
143   Wikipedia: Prince Shōtoku. ibid.
144   Wikipedia: Sugawara no Michizane. Online at http://en.wikipedia.org/wiki/Sugawara_no_Michizane
145   Wikipedia: Taira no Masakado. Online at http://en.wikipedia.org/wiki/Taira_no_Masakado
146   Wikipedia: Minamoto no Yoshitsune. Online at http://en.wikipedia.org/wiki/Minamoto_no_Yoshitsune
147   Wikipedia: Forty-seven Ronin. Online at http://en.wikipedia.org/wiki/Forty-seven_Ronin
148   Wikipedia: Edo period. Online at http://en.wikipedia.org/wiki/Edo_period

archipelago, particularly among common people who lived in big cities.

Nevertheless, the spirits of these individuals were viewed as dangerous and harmful to living humans, since they all ended their lives tragically and sometimes cursing the world. Therefore, they were considered as the subject's pacification either through Buddhist or Shinto religious ceremonies, according to the explanation of Umehara study. People continued the practice throughout centuries because they feared the curse and vengeance. Those who lived after the death of these individuals did so either immediately after or long after the time that the departure took place.

The appeasements were often made by rulers or those in positions of authority and sometimes by commoners or lower class people with no power. However, all of them were fearful of disasters such as epidemics, earthquakes or famines caused by the angry spirits of these who suffered tragic death. Rulers were usually afraid of rebellions, the rise of their oppositions and unstable political circumstances. Peasants and common people in cities were more afraid of famines and natural disasters such as earthquakes, volcanic eruptions and tsunami. They did so because both rulers and commoners in the country firmly believed in the existence of the ghosts, spiritual world and life after death during the medieval ages.

Another example of the application of the belief in avenging sprits is that of Shotoku Taishi, or Prince Shotoku, a regent, the son of Emperor Yōmei[149] who died in 587, and a nephew of Empress Suiko (554-628)[150]. Under his leadership

---

149   Wikipedia: Emperor Yōmei. Online at http://en.wikipedia.org/wiki/Emperor_Yomei_of_Japan
150   Wikipedia: Empress Suiko. Online at http://en.wikipedia.org/wiki/Empress_Suiko

the country made the great transformation to a civilized nation-state and the centralized Imperial state system, introducing Buddhism, Confucianism and Taoism from China as well as sciences and technologies. His drastic reforms laid the foundations for the Japanese legal system and administrative structure.

However, there are many mysteries regarding the end of his political career and life. Despite his mother came from ruling Soga family[151] with possible Chinese lineage and great political influence to the imperial court during most of his life, the Soga family had a sharp decline and lost their power around the time of Shotoku's death. According to the historical record, the Soga family was massacred when a bloody coup d'état took place in the capital of Nara in 645 A.D. Children of Prince Shotoku were banished shortly after the coup which eliminated the entire clan. Umehara also contends that the bloody massacre in the palace in Nara conceived many mysteries[152]. The coup d'état was plotted by the members of newly rising Nakatomi clan[153] that was about to replace the ruling Soga clan of Prince Shokuto's sweeping reforms.

The Nakatomi clan assassinated Soga no Iruka[154] the clan leader and close ally of the prince and other family members. Umehara argues that 25 descendents of Prince Shotoku could have been murdered by the new ruling family shortly before the bloody incident in the capital and strongly disagrees with the statement by Nihonshoki that makes Soga no Iruka responsible for their deaths. The newly risen ruling oligarchy,

---

151   Wikipedia: 蘇我氏. Online at http://ja.wikipedia.org/wiki/%E8%98%87%E6%88%91%E6%B0%8F

152   Umehara. ibid.

153   Wikipedia: Nakatomi clan. Online at http://en.wikipedia.org/wiki/Nakatomi_clan

154   Wikipedia: 蘇我入鹿. Online at http://en.wikipedia.org/wiki/Soga_no_Iruka

according to Umehara, plotted to eliminate both Soga no Iruka and those descended from the prince. Strangely enough, offsprings of Shotoku disappeared around the time of this massacre.

After the time of Prince Shotoku, the appeasement of vengeful spirits following Buddhist sutra became more prevalent than the traditional Shinto method. But Shinto priests did not give up their role as pacifiers of angry spirits for new teachings from the continent, and remained still active in it.

Sugawara-no-Michizane is another example of one whose spirit was appeased in the Shinto way, although Buddhism was already spread throughout the nation in his days. Michizane was a scholar, poet, and politician of the Heian Period of Japan. He was an extremely talented individual who worked for the government office. Because of the extraordinary talent, he was once promoted to a minister's position by Emperor Uda (867–931)[155].

However, he had very unhappy ending in both his career and personal life. After the passing of the emperor who was in favor of Michizane, his position became increasingly shaky and vulnerable. He was demoted from the government minister's rank in Kyoto to a minor official post at Dazaifu, in Kyushu's Chikuzen Province. It was near to exile for him, since he was separated from all of his close friends and colleagues in Kyoto. Michizane died in the Chikuzen Province in desperation and with a sense of betrayal. The legend says that the Great Audience Hall of the Imperial Palace was struck repeatedly

---

155   Wikipedia: 宇多天皇. Online at http://ja.wikipedia.org/wiki/%E5%AE%87%E5%A4%9A%E5%A4%A9%E7%9A%87

by lightning, and the city of Kyoto experienced weeks of rainstorms and floods after his death[156].

The government officials decided to appease the angry spirit of Michizane with the belief that Michizane's angry spirit caused natural disasters and the death of the emperor's sons. In order to relieve the angry spirit of the exiled Michizane, the imperial court built a Shinto shrine called Kitano Tenman-gū in Kyoto, and dedicated it to him. Because of this he was deified as *Tenjin-sama*, or Kami of scholarship in a shrine called Tenman-gu[157]. He was also known as a patron for students like Saint Nicholas in the West because he endeavored to support students during his academic and political career. After his lonely death during his exile in Dazaifu, plague and drought spread and two sons of Emperor Daigo died. It seems that the posthumous status as Kami and resultant fame of Sugawara-no-Michizane were endowed to him by those who were afraid of his vengeance.

Another example is Taïra-no-Masakado,[158] a warlord who belonged to the Taira clan[159] descended from Emperor Kammu (737–806)[160] and who lived during the Heian Period. He was a landowner in the Kantō region. He was defeated and died after leading large insurgent forces against the central government in Kyoto. He was very popular among peasant class folks in his own district and considered as a hero who declared war against the corrupted imperial court. People in the central government, however, regarded him as a criminal

156   Wikipedia: Sugawara no Michizane. ibid.
157   Ebihara. Shinto War Gods of Yasukuni Shrine. ibid.
158   Wikipedia: Taira no Masakado. ibid.
159   Wikipedia: Taira clan (平氏). Online at http://en.wikipedia.org/wiki/Taira
160   Wikipedia: Emperor Kammu (桓武天皇). Online at http://en.wikipedia.org/wiki/
Emperor_Kammu

who disturbed the peace. After his death, his head was removed from his body and transported to Kyoto where it was displayed in public. According to the legend, his head flew over to the east and fell on the wilderness in the district of current day Tokyo. People there started worshipping the dead hero as a god and built a Shinto shrine named *Kanda-myōjin* (神田明神) which meant "god of enlightenment in Kanda"[161] or Kanda Shrine.

His action had split the public opinion over the course of Japanese history. Those who are loyal to the imperial family consistently disapprove his actions because he called himself a "new emperor" appointed by the heavenly force. For them, the imperial lineage that descended from the sun-goddess Amaterasu is sacred and inviolable. Therefore an attempt to start a new monarchy or take over the throne from the direct lineage from the sun-goddess is outrageous and blasphemous. However, for those who do not care for what they consider the imperial myth, his actions were legitimate and even heroic, since the court during the Heian Period was corrupted. Masakado was descended from an emperor, although his family was outside of the court for several generations. Therefore, many of his contemporaries believed he had a right to be installed into the throne legitimately.

Although Masakado was not an ancestor of samurai-class rulers which emerged in the next era, the myth was a convenient tool for them to undermine the imperial authority. Particularly, Tokugawa shogunate which came into existence in the 17th century, took advantage of the Masakado myth and Kanda-myōjin to weaken the emperor's power.

---

161   Wikipedia: Kanda Shrine. Online at http://en.wikipedia.org/wiki/Kanda_Shrine

Shogun was practically a Japanese monarchy for longer and more respected than the emperor, although his technical social status was lower than the court officials. However, the emperor was not totally powerless during a long period of the imperial dormancy. The emperor still possessed power to authorize offices, appoint, promote or demote people who worked there. Shogun was deeply in trouble if the emperor promoted his adversary into a higher position than himself. Because of this, Japanese rulers during centuries after Heian Period were very cautious about the emperor.

Kanda-myōjin was a very popular shrine among commoners during Edo Period when the emperor's power was dormant and almost invisible. It developed a rivalry against Kyoto and the imperial court during this period and developed a deep awe and respect to the hero who boldly challenged their rival.

Kanda-myōjin during centuries played two ambivalent and opposing roles. For those in the court and central government, it existed for the sake of pacifying the angry ghost of Taïra-no-Masakado a warlord who rebelled against the imperial court. However, for those outside of the government structure, particularly in Tokyo area where his rebellion actually happened, it was a place to empower people to fight against corrupted leaders, since Masakado was a Kami who could liberate them from the oppression of rulers in any ages.

The Tokugawa shogunate[162] government officials also encouraged common people in the city of Edo to worship Masakado who rebelled against the imperial authority because

---

162   Wikipedia: Tokugawa shogunate. Online at http://en.wikipedia.org/wiki/Tokugawa_Shogunate

they tried to reduce the emperor's authority as much as they could. They had to diminish the power of the emperor, because Tokugawa's adversaries could use imperial authority to rise against it. It was a unique situation that the Tokugawa shogunate took advantage of the cursing power of vengeful spirit to suppress the emperor's authority.

However, Tokugawa shogunite government never tried to overthrow the emperor or become another emperor himself. During long history of Japan, no one tried to eliminate the imperial system or take over that position except Taïra-no-Masakado.

Minamoto-no-Yoshitsune[163] was another individual who suffered a tragic death, and whose soul required appeasement according to Umehara. He was a warlord who lived in the late Heian and early Kamakura period, born as the ninth son of Minamoto no Yoshitomo who was the chief of the Minamoto clan[164] descended from an emperor like Taira clan. Yoshitsune is well known for his extraordinary military prowess and is an extremely popular historical figure of his era. He was born shortly before the Heiji Rebellion of 1159 in which his father and oldest two brothers died. After his father was killed, his oldest half-brother Yoshihira was captured and beheaded by members of Taira clan[165] newly ascended to the rulership. The legend states that Yoshihira became a thunder god after his departure and struck the executer to death with lightening while his head was displayed in the city of Kyoto.

---

163   Wikipedia: Minamoto no Yoshitsune. Online at http://en.wikipedia.org/wiki/Minamoto_no_Yoshitsune

164   Wikipedia: Minamoto clan. Online at http://en.wikipedia.org/wiki/Minamoto

165   Wikipedia: Taira clan. ibid.

According to historians, both Yoshitomo and Yoshihira were extremely powerful warriors with tremendous military expertise but also had rude, crude and cruel social behavior and had excessively aggressive and violent temperaments.

According to the legend, Tengu (天狗)[166] in Mount Kurama taught Yoshitsune sword art and raised him to be a great warrior. After he grew up to adulthood, he joined the army of Minamoto no Yoritomo[167] one of his older half-brothers and the new head of the Minamoto clan defeated the Taira clan. After defeating the largest enemy and his father's foe, he joined the cloistered Emperor Go-Shirakawa (1127-1192)[168] and plotted against his brother Yoritomo. However, Go-Shirakawa betrayed Yoshitsune after learning Yoritomo's political power was much more powerful than he thought. There was also a big earthquake in Kyoto which utterly destroyed the capital and deprived the morale of the imperial warriors. Fleeing to the temporary protection of Fujiwara no Hidehira in the Tohoku area of Northern Japan, Yoshitsune was betrayed there again by Hidehira who was afraid of overpowering force of Yoritomo. It is generally believed that he was defeated and committed suicide along with his wife and children, although the very end of his life remains a mystery.

Go-Shirakawa was an extremely sly, crafty and snake like former emperor with exceptional skills of deceptios. He attempted to play one military or Samurai class clan against another, hoping to maintain the prestige and power of the imperial court. First, he supported the Taira clan, then changed

---

166   Wikipedia: Tengu. ibid.
167   Wikipedia: Minamoto no Yoritomo (源頼朝). Online at http://en.wikipedia.org/wiki/Minamoto_no_Yoritomo
168   Wikipedia: Emperor Go-Shirakawa (後白河). Online at http://en.wikipedia.org/wiki/Emperor_Go-Shirakawa

his side and supported Yoritomo when Tairas became the ruling oligarchy. Taïras became too strong and no longer listened to him. He attempted a coup d'état to expel *Taïra-no-Kiyomori* (1118 – 1181)[169], the clan leader of Heike, but failed. Then, Yoritomo, the third son of the late Minamoto no Yoshitomo consolidated his home base in Kamakura (鎌倉) near today's Tokyo. Goshirakawa supported Yoritomo and other newly rising Samurai Class rulers to defeat the Taïra Clan. Yoritomo, Yoshitsune and other members of the Minamoto clan united together and defeated a Taïra oligarchy. However, Go-Shirakawa did not want Minamotos to overpower the imperial court, so he assisted Yoshitsune to assemble a force against Yoritomo's army, trying to undermine Yoritomo's leadership in Kamakura. His attempt failed, but he managed to escape from backlash or blame from Yoritomo's camp. He exercised skills to imply whether or not he was supporting rebellions so that he could elude the backfire if a rebellion failed. Such exquisite skills to elude blame and responsibility has been passed down to the imperial family throughout the generations. Later, Yoritomo nicknamed Go-Shirakawa as the "greatest Tengu of the nation of Japanese"[170] because of his pride, puffed up ego, skills of deception and elusiveness.

The real Minamoto-no-Yoshitsune as a historical figure shared the same kind of temperament and personality as his father and oldest half-brother. He possessed a great military prowess like Yamato Takeru or Samson in the Old Testament and many other illustrious heroes all over the world, but minimum social skills and academics. However, a long time

---

169   Wikipedia: Taira no Kiyomori (平清盛). Online at http://en.wikipedia.org/wiki/Taira_no_Kiyomori

170   Tengu is often used as a symbol of pride and conceited ego from the antiquity.

after his death Yoshitsune's image was gradually transformed into a man of character, seen as a genteel, kind, educated and refined individual by many who lived in the later age period and admired him as a hero who suffered a tragic death. These Yoshitsune fans made him into a perfect, ideal and most admirable person quite apart from the Minamoto-no-Yoshitsune in the real Japanese history.

On the other hand, unlike most others in Minamoto clan, Yoritomo was considered a genius of politics with excellent social and academic skills although his military ability was just average. His mother was a daughter of a Shinto priest from a prestigious shrine, so that he was well versed in aristocratic social manners. Because of his social graces and political skills that all other members of the Minamoto clan did not possess, he became a Samurai class ruler of Japan. However, until the death of Go-Shirakawa, Yoritomo was unable to obtain the imperial commission as *Sei-i tai shogun* (征夷大将軍), a title widely known as *Shogun*, a position which carried practically dictatorial powers and which he ardently desired both for its prestige and practical advantage.

Almost all Yoshitsune fans are not in favor of Yoritomo and consistently view him as an extremely crafty, sly, cold-blooded ruler who only cared about himself. However, most historians agreed that Yoritomo did not have the sole responsibility for Yoshitsune's death, since he was tightly controlled by the Hōjō clan and other ruling families in Kamakura. Yoritomo had to work hard to meet desires and wishes of these people, because they were vital supporters of the regime who might determine his destiny and political life in the future. It seemed that Yoshitsune and Yoritomo's other half-brothers that joined the force were not in favor of these in the ruling class of Kamakura, since they were all eliminated at the end.

Those from Hōjō and other local clans acted like Yoritomo's loyal vassal. However, they viewed their master as no more than an instrument to bring them a wealth or at best an equal comrade who shared practical advantages with them. Kamakura did not welcome these crude and simplistic half-brothers of Yoritomo, because they did not possess enough social and political skills to woo and win the favor of the local rulers and provide them practical advantages. Some scholars even argue that Yoritomo could also have been assassinated by the Hōjō family when he lost the practical value for them, since his death was somehow mysterious, but there seems to be no actual evidence for this.

There are only few a Buddhist temples or Shinto shrines dedicated to Yoshitsune, since he was not originally considered a vengeful soul when he died. There was no national project to appease his spirit because so many warriors in his days suffered similar kinds of death and rulers did not find pressing needs to do so. However, Gikeiji Temple (義経寺) in Aomori prefecture is one of few temples dedicated to him. According to the most accepted view about his death, Yoshitsune committed "seppuku" when he was seized by the force of Fujiwara no Hidehira.

However, the legend around the Gikeiji says that Yoshitsune fled to Hokkaido (北海道) the northernmost island which did not belong to Japan during the mediaeval age[171]. Betrayed by both the former emperor Go-Shirakawa and

_____

171   義経北行伝説の足跡を追う: ま ほ ろ ば LAND, 2002. Online at http:// homepage1.nifty.com/maholobaland/yositune/gikeiji.htm

Fujiwara no Hidehira, he was experiencing a tremendous crisis, but did not take his life. Instead, he placed a small Kwannon[172] statue on a rock near the shore, and prayed to it for three days and nights. Finally, an old man with a white beard appeared and gave him a *ryoma* (龍馬) or "dragon horse" suggesting that he should flee to Hokkaido across the channel. The legend says that Yoshitsune and his party travelled to the the northernmost island following the advice of a mysterious man. Local people in the same district discovered the Kwannon statue Yoshitsune left in order to demonstrate the appreciation of divine power. They built the Gikeiji Temple to honor the great hero who fled to the north following the guidance of Kwannon.

In Hokkaido, there are many different Yoshitsune legends among the Ainu or aboriginal population there, although the historicity of these stories is questionable. These tales tell that he helped the Ainu[173] people greatly by teaching them agriculture and other skills and sciences. However, most scholars agree that these stories were created during the Edo Period when Japanese started immigration to Hokkaido. Scholars say that Yoshitsune legends were convenient tools for Tokugawa shogunate government to integrate the Ainu into the Japanese population and take over the land safely.

There is also a somewhat absurd but entertaining story that Yoshitsune went further north with his followers and arrived at Mongolia. People in Mongolia welcomed him for his extraordinary military skills, installed him as the emperor and named him *Genghis Khan* (1162 – 1227)[174]. Siebold (1796 – 1866), one of the leading Japanologists in the 19th century,

---

172   Kwannon: Encyclo Online Encyclopedia. Ibid.
173   Wikipedia: Ainu people. Online at http://en.wikipedia.org/wiki/Ainu_people
174   Wikipedia: Genghis Khan. Online at http://en.wikipedia.org/wiki/Genghis_Khan

noted that his Japanese friend Yoshio Tadajiro was convinced that Yoshitsune was identical to Genghis Khan[175]. People who created this legend likely because both Yoshitsune and Genghis Khan were military geniuses[176]. During the Kamakura Period, *Kubilai Khan* (1215 – 1294), the grandson of Genghis Khan, did send a navy fleet to Japan and the invasion force almost landed. A huge rain storm, however, wiped out the invaders, and the Japanese called that storm *Kamikaze* or "divine wind".

During the time the Mongolian attack happened, the Minamoto shogunate that descended from Yoritomo was already extinct, and the Hōjō clan, the most powerful ruling families in Kamakura, took over the leadership. The leadership of Kamakura by the Hōjō family was as corrupt as the imperial court, and both overtaxed the population. The commoners during these days suffered greatly through paying taxes to both parties. It is understandable that the common people equated the raging Mongolian invasion force with the vengeful spirit of Minamoto-no-Yoshitsune murdered by the rulers of Kamakura. They might have viewed that Kubilai Khan the Mongol emperor sent a fleet to Kamakura to punish the rulers from both Minamoto and Hōjō clan and avenge his grandfather or late Great Minamoto-no-Yoshitsune. The invasion of the Mongolian force failed because of a heavy rain storm. It is not certain when people created the legend that Yoshitsune became the founder of the Mongol Empire. However, if it already existed during the time of Mongol invasion, Japanese rulers might have

175   Philipp Franz Von Siebold. Manners and Customs of the Japanese in the Nineteenth Century: From the Accounts of Dutch Residents in Japan and from the German Work of Philipp Franz (Charleston, SC, USA: Nabu Press, 1832/2010)

176   義経＝ジンギスカン伝説を追う：おおさかページ, 2007. Online at http://www.library.pref.osaka.jp/nakato/shotenji/19_yoshi.html

been convinced of the pressing need to appease the spirit of Minamoto-no-Yoshitsune.

People who live in the Hokkaido region associate one of their gourmet specialities with Mongolia. They call it *Genghis Khan Nabe* and it is barbecue beef, chicken, lamb and vegetables on a big frying pan. All of that goes back to Minamoto-no-Yoshitsune and the Mongol invasion.

The 47 Samurai of Ako[177] who had been put to death during the Edo Period were additional historic figures to be appeased according to Umehara study. The story tells of a group of samurai avenged of their master Asano Takumi no Kami (1667 – 1701) who was forced to commit *seppuku* for assaulting a court official named Kira Kōzuke no suke. They launched a raid on Kira's compound in the city of Edo and decapitated him after patiently waiting and planning for two years. After the raid, they marched around the city with the head of Kira and celebrated. Shortly after that, they were placed into custody and forced to commit seppuku for committing the crime of murder.

Both these warriors and their master were put to death, since they broke the law and committed violent crimes. Nevertheless, the general public during those days was very sympathetic to these samurai and approved their action, since the shogunate government was extremely corrupt. People during the Edo Period viewed Kira Kōzuke no suke as a notoriously corrupt individual, so that they had little sympathy for him though he was brutally murdered.

---

177   Wikipedia: Forty-seven Ronin. Online at http://en.wikipedia.org/wiki/Forty-seven_Ronin

Noh & Kabuki Theatre to Pacify Vengeful Spirits

Noh (能)[178] and *Kabuki* (歌舞伎)[179] are well known traditional theatrical arts in today's Japan which, according to Umehara, carry an important theme of vengeful spirits in their performances. The former is a classical musical drama that has been performed since the 14th century and is characterized by various masks containing symbolical expressions of human emotions. The performance consists of singing and dancing and the message to the audience is obtusely codified. Therefore, *Noh* is generally considered the theater of symbols, and requires some background knowledge to decode the underlined message. Umehara also includes the main character that holds an avenging spirit of a dead within[180]. According to Umehara:

> It is instead the theater of avenging spirits, these being the most important characters. In the Noh theater of Zeami, great creator of this dramatic art form, the *shite* (protagonist) nearly always represents one of the spirits, and the *waki* (secondary character) is relatively unimportant. The *shite*, incarnation of an avenging spirit, appears before the waki in a form invisible to men, the *ai*. At the same time the spirits always appear in their normal human forms. In other words the spirits acquire a double dimension: they are themselves and at the same time those who hide from the sight of living men.

The theatre was originally started around the 14th century and significantly developed by Zeami Motokiyo (1363 – 1443)[181] an artist, actor and playwright in the Muromachi

---

178   Wikipedia: Noh. Online at http://en.wikipedia.org/wiki/Noh
179   Wikipedia: Kabuki. Online at http://en.wikipedia.org/wiki/Kabuki
180   Umehara. Ibid.
181   Wikipedia: 世阿弥元清. Online at http://ja.wikipedia.org/wiki/%E4%B8%96%E9%98%BF%E5%BC%A5

period (室町時代)[182]. He was trained and educated in acting by his father who was also a performer. He also received a court education in the arts later in his life after being recognized for his exceptional talent by Ashikaga Yoshimitsu (1358 – 1408)[183] a very powerful shogunate ruler. Upon the passing of his father, Zeami succeeded the family business and developed his own style of theatrical art which integrated the performance with Buddhist religiosity. He created many dramatic literatures in which the protagonists were ghosts of various historical and fictional characters who suffered painful deaths. He wrote several stories of women who suffered painful death and transformed into Hannya (般若)[184] or female Oni (鬼)[185] because of their jealousy and vengeful thoughts. However, the souls of these angry women are pacified by the power of *Hannya-Shin-Kyo* (般若心経)[186] or *Prajñā-pāramitā-hrdaya,* their sacred sūtra, which carries a power to pacify angry spirits and demonic forces according to the medieval Buddhist belief.

Later, Zeami's theatre became a great success, since his extraordinary talent bloomed and rapidly lifted him to celebrity status. Although he had a humble background as a drama performer's son far below the nobility, his theatrical themes and style were understood well and widely favoured by aristocratic audiences. Having received support and patronage from shoguns, including Ashikaga Yoshimitsu and many other aristocrats, Zeami proved his genius as a performer and theatrical artist. He made a great success for his esoteric,

---

182   Wikipedia: Muromachi period. Online at http://en.wikipedia.org/wiki/Muromachi_period

183   Wikipedia: 足利義満. ibid.

184   Wikipedia: Hannya (般若). ibid.

185   Wikipedia: Oni (folklore). ibid.

186   Wikipedia: 般若心経. Online at http://ja.wikipedia.org/wiki/%E8%88%AC%E8%8B%A5%E5%BF%83%E7%B5%8C

otherworldly themes based on the Buddhist philosophy and established his name in Japanese history. The social religious background during this period in which the Buddhist belief system permeated the entire Japanese society, likely contributed to his great success.

Using Martin Heidegger's (1889 – 1976)[187] theory of "being" as an analogy, Umehara explains the dynamics of the *Noh* theatre, in which the shite or the protagonist is the host or a living person who holds another man's ghost inside of him. Heidegger had a discussion on the internal and existential true ego who resides inside of our flesh or external self[188]. Umehara applied the same method to separate internal and external self to explain the internal psyche of *Noh's* protagonist. The host gradually unveils the existential man or the spirit of the dead which resides within his body. According to him, the *shite* or the protagonist is a living person with an ordinary look has another personality within or the spirit of a dead who suffered a painful death. It is fascinating that the ghost of the dead takes over the body of another person, and starts acting like the super-ego within revealing his or her painful and vengeful thoughts to the audience throughout the performance of Zeami's *Noh* theatre.

Waki is the secondary character with an appearance of being less important, but who in reality plays a very significant role to pacify the angry spirit. He is going to bring out the spirit residing in the host by asking him questions in the same way as psychotherapists do to their patients. Umehara contends

187   Wikipedia: Martin Heidegger. Online at http://en.wikipedia.org/wiki/Martin_ Heidegger
188   Martin Heidegger. Being and Time. (New York City, NY: USA: Harper Perennial Modern Classics, 1927/2008)

that in the climax of the performance the *shite* finally unveils his true personality through increasingly rapid and staccato music and dance. Umehara continues his discussion that when the *shite* reaches the peak of insanity and nears the culmination of his revelation, the *waki* changes from a spectator to an exorcist with a vital role to neutralize the angry spirit. In order to pacify the spirit and complete the entire process of the exorcism releasing him or her to the afterworld, waki the high priest appeals to the "inner power of Buddhist truth" that every human subject possesses according to their philosophy.

Buddhists believe that the spirit of the dead can possess a living person and take over his body in the same way as demons in the Christian worldview. Umehara came to the conclusion that Zeami acted as a high priest of avenging spirits by creating a theatre. He summons spirits to the stage and allows them to express their sorrows and anger, and finally discharges them to the world of the dead when appeasement is completed.

Kabuki is another theatrical tradition in Japan which came into existence in the Edo Period. Unlike *Noh*, the performance does not include masks and the message to the audience is more explicit. Therefore, the background knowledge or key to decode the message is not necessary. The Kabuki performance consists of singing and dancing like Noh, and Umehara (1974) observes that it derived from Noh having inherited the same theatrical theme of appeasing the spirits[189].

The target audiences of Kabuki were commoners or city dwellers of Edo, while the Noh theatre originally targeted

---

189   Umehara. Ibid.

nobles of the imperial court and Samurai class rulers. Because of this, most protagonists in Kabuki are popular heroes who suffer tragic deaths and earn fame and sympathy among common people, just as Sugawara-no-Michizane, Taïra-no-Masakado, Minamoto-no-Yoshitsune, and the 47 "ronins" of Ako. Commoners in the city of Edo were sympathetic to these individuals, since they all were put to death, more or less directly, by those in power. Their preference for the tragic heroes might also reflect their own sense of powerlessness in front of cruel and tyrannical rulers, since Edo society was far apart from the democracy in the modern world.

In the Edo period when Kabuki came into existence, Minamoto-no-Yoshitsune was considered a vengeful soul who required appeasement. Furthermore, the Tokugawa shogunate government had started colonizing Hokkaido.

However, they did not approve the performance of 47 Samurai of Ako since it was very current and carried touchy subjects for the government. Kabuki theatre had to use pseudonymous for the real people who were involved in this incident, as they created a scenario for the performance. The story of 47 Samurai of Ako became gradually popular during the Edo period, and now is a part of popular entertainment culture outside of the Kabuki theatre. This story is widely liked by the general public because vengeance is a favorite motif among Japanese.

Precisely speaking, these 47 warriors were not individuals who required appeasement according to both Buddhist and Shinto teachings, since they avenged of their master Asano

Takumi no Kami by taking the head of his nemeses *Kira Kōzuke no suke*. Although these Samurai warriors were taken into custody after the incident and ordered to commit seppuku, they were allowed to die in the most honorable way. They could die with honor, since Tokugawa Tsunayoshi (1646-1709)[190] the Shogun who reigned over Japan during the time that the raid took place, and other officials were quite sympathetic to these warriors and gave them maximum favor. Both common people and rulers acknowledged that Kira Kōzuke no suke was a very corrupt and infamous individual, so that he deserved death or an extremely severe punishment. Probably, the Shogun and other government leaders were also afraid of being exposed to criticism from the public for not having punished Kira before the incident happened.

Therefore, they must have no regret and there was no reason that they become vengeful ghosts according to the Buddhist hermeneutic. However, many temples all over the country continue annual ceremonies to comfort these Samurai over centuries. The most famous ceremonies concerning these warriors take place at Sengakuji (泉岳寺) in Tokyo, where they were buried along with their master Asano. The temple carries out the ceremony dedicated to them in April and December twice in a year.

There are many other Buddhist temples in Tokyo and Kyoto performing the same kind of commemorations for these Samurai warriors and many local residents and tourists also attend these functions. They continue these ceremonies probably because the majority of Japanese citizens still view these individuals as heroic, since they have successfully

---

190   Wikipedia: Tokugawa Tsunayoshi (徳川綱吉). Online at http://en.wikipedia.org/wiki/Tokugawa_Tsunayoshi

avenged their master. Unlike most Westerners, the average Japanese does not regard forgiveness of his or her own emesis or perpetrator as a moral obligation, since they still praise the motif of vengeance.

Haunting Spirit of Taira Clan

Lafcadio Hearn[191] lived in the 19th century and did an in-depth study of Japanese culture, spirituality and the world of yokai and ghosts after immigrating to Japan from Britain. He wrote a fascinating short story in which the main character is "Mimi-Nashi-Hoichi" or earless Hoichi, a genius musician who was haunted by ghosts of Taïra clan and a child emperor Antoku (1178 – 1185)[192] who died with them. After Taira clan was driven out of Kyoto by the army of Minamoto-no-Yoshitsune[193], Antoku left the Kyoto together with them, since his grandfather on his mother's side was Taïra-no-Kiyomori[194] the chief of the clan. First, Kiyomori made one of his daughters the empress of the former emperor Takakura (1161 - 1181), and waited until their baby son Antoku arrived. Antoku was installed to the throne as an infant, since Kiyomori wanted to siege the court and stabilize his regime by making his grandson an emperor.

Hoichi is a blind musician during the Kamakura Period who specialized in playing the *biwa*, a four-stringed lute, and reciting passages of poems and stories. He belongs to the professionals called *biwa-hoshi* or "lute priest" who travels around the country and play the biwa and recites stories, mainly the Tale of the Heike, an epic account of the strife

---

191   Wikipedia: Lafcadio Hearn. ibid.
192   Wikipedia: Emperor Antoku (安徳天皇). Online at http://en.wikipedia.org/wiki/Antoku
193   Wikipedia: Minamoto no Yoshitsune. ibid.
194   Wikipedia: Taira no Kiyomori. Ibid.

between the Taïra and Minamoto clans. The original objective of the lute priests when the profession came into existence was to pacify the souls of dead soldiers. But their performance became a popular entertainment during this period.

Hoici has trouble with ghosts of the Taïra clan because he has performed the music and recitation too well[195]. Ghosts of Samurai warriors supposedly dead after being defeated by Yoshitsune in the battle of Dan-no-Ura, approach Hoichi for his excellent performance. In this story, ghost of neither Taïra-no-Kiyomori nor any other prominent person from the Taïra clan is present. Hoichi can hear only a voice of unnamed Samurai warrior and a woman and so seduced into dangerous territory which is haunted, he has to play biwa and recite the story of *Dan-no-Ura* from the *Tale of the Heike* in front of ghosts of the warriors and their emperor.

Hoichi starts the performance every night in the same location after he has been recruited by ghosts. The priest of the temple where Hoichi is staying is an old friend and begins to realize that Hoichi's attitude and behavior have changed. He becomes concerned with Hoichi's strange behavior and suspicious of his nightly outings. So the priest sends his servants to follow and spy on him as he leaves the temple one rainy night. Hoichi walks extremely fast for a blind man in a rainy night, and the men lost him. However, they start hearing a beautiful tune of biwa from the direction of the graveyard of Emperor Antoku. Then, they walk to the cemetery and see that the young lute priest is playing biwa and reciting a story in front of tomb stones where no audience is present. He is playing

---

195   Lafcadio Hearn. Kwaidan. (North Clarendon, VT: USA: Tuttle Publishing, 1904/1971)

music and singing or screaming at tomb stones like a mad man there.

They tell him that he must come home with them because he is bewitched. He responds by telling them, "To interrupt me in such manner, before this august assembly, will not be tolerated". These servants cannot help laughing, since they find no august or respectful and magnificent assembly of people in front of him. Because they come to the conclusion that he was really bewitched, they seize him, pull him up on his feet and carry him back to the temple. The priest orders his servants to relieve Hoichi of his wet clothes, re-clothe him and have him eat and drink[196].

Though Hoichi hesitates to speak about it, the priest demands an explanation of his strange behavior and the entire incident. Finally, he starts telling him reluctantly everything that has happened from the time he encounters a strange Samurai the first time. Then, the priest learns that his friend is in a grave danger and tells him not to visit them again[197]. Then, he gives Hoichi a suggestion that:

> All that you have been imagining was illusion — except the calling of the dead. By once obeying them, you have put yourself in their power. If you obey them again, after what has already occurred, they will tear you in pieces. But they would have destroyed you, sooner or later, in any event. Now, I shall not be able to remain with you to-night: I am called away to perform another service. But, before I go, it will be necessary to protect your body by writing holy text upon it.

These spirits were human ghosts transformed into Yōkai (妖怪)[198] by some sort of extreme emotional state such as grief,

---

196   Hearn. Kwaidan. ibid.
197   Hearn. Kwaidan. ibid.
198   Wikipedia: Yōkai. ibid.

intense jealousy, rage, wrath, pain or vengeful thoughts and lost humanity. The priest was afraid that they might tear Hoichi in pieces at any time because they are not humans any more. The sacred text that the priest mentioned was *Hannya-Shin-Kyo* (般若心経)[199] or *Prajñā-pāramitā-hrdaya, a sūtra*, which carries a power to pacify angry spirits and demonic forces according to the medieval Buddhists belief. It was a text that Murasaki Shikibu[200] and Zeami[201] quoted when vengeful spirits were being appeased. It was also used in a real ceremony to appease vengeful spirits of individuals who suffered a painful death. People who lived in medieval Japan believed in the magical power of the sūtra to drive out of vengeful spirits and demons from the domain of the living.

Returning to the story of *Mimi-Nashi-Hoichi*, the priest orders his acolyte to write the sacred text on the entire body of the young lute priest, so that he is protected from the angry spirits of Samurai warriors of the Taïra clan and Emperor Antoku. When the priest is about to leave the temple with his acolyte, he gives Hoichi the following instruction.

> Tonight, as soon as I go away, you must seat yourself on the verandah, and wait. You will be called. But, whatever may happen, do not answer, and do not move. Say nothing, and sit still — as if meditating. If you stir, or make any noise, you will be torn asunder.

After dark, he and his acolyte leave the temple for an engagement. When Hoichi is left alone on the verandah, he hears again the ghosts of Samurai warriors calling him in a deep voice. Following the instruction given by the priest, he sits

199   Wikipedia: 般若心経. ibid.
200   Wikipedia: Murasaki Shikibu. ibid.
201   Wikipedia: 世阿弥. Online at http://ja.wikipedia.org/wiki/%E4%B8%96%E9%98%BF%E5%BC%A5

still, motionless, holding his breath and never responding to the voice. Because of the sacred sūtra written on his body, they find biwa, but not the player. However, only his ears are visible to them because the acolyte has forgotten to write a text on them. One of the ghosts ripped them off from his body, saying, "Now, to my lord these ears I will take in proof that the august commands has been obeyed[202]". The priest and acolyte come back to see Hoichi bleeding, his ears ripped off and indignant that the acolyte forgot to write the sacred sūtra on his ears. However, he is also pleased that the crisis is over and these ghosts are no more pursuing him.

It appears odd that the character of Emperor Antoku was absent in Hearn's story, although he was supposedly the master of these ghosts. After being recruited by the ghost of Samurai warrior, Hoichi was supposed to play biwa and recite the story of Dan-no-Ura for his master or the late Emperor Antoku. However, Hearn did not describe Hoichi meeting the emperor or even his presence during the entire story.

This could have been because of Japanese government policies during the Meiji Period (1868 - 1912)[203]. Hearn had to comply to the standpoint which regards Japanese emperor as "sacred and inviolable". The Meiji Government invented *Kokutai* (国体, lit. national essence/entity/polity)[204], an ideological system and "moral concept that constituted the very essence of the state" around the emperor system. It was the ideological system based on the supreme authority of the emperor as the inviolable high priest or spiritual head of the nation. In this ideological system, the entire state was a unitary

---

202   Hearn. Kwaidan. ibid.
203   Wikipedia: Meiji period. Online at http://en.wikipedia.org/wiki/Meiji_period
204   Wikipedia: Kokutai. Online at http://en.wikipedia.org/wiki/Kokutai

sacro-society or form of cultic religious community that involved the emperor, government and all citizens or subjects of the country[205].

Under this system, any individual with disrespectful attitudes or conduct to the emperor and his family either in contemporary or ancient days was prosecuted and severely punished. In those days, the Japanese government did not tolerate literature in which anyone from the imperial family, including historical characters, are described as a vengeful spirit and cursing the world. Hearn had to do his job under a strict restriction because he was one of the government employees who taught English at the Tokyo Imperial University (東京帝国大学).

Following the storyline of *Mimi-Nashi-Hoichi*, Antoku was supposedly transformed into Yōkai[206], a preternatural creature in Japanese folklore and mythological world when he was drowned with his vassals of the Taïra clan. If Hearn was going to describe the character of the emperor as the lord of darkness, he would have had to have been the very eerie head of the vampire like creatures. At the end of the story, he would be very pleased to receive severed ears of the poor lute priest gravely offered by one of the vassals saying "Job well-done". Such a story might be entertaining for many readers in the Meiji Period. However, if the "sacred and inviolable" emperor was described as a bloodthirsty chief of spooky ghosts, the Meiji government would not tolerate Hearn's story. At best, Hearn might have lost his job. In a worst scenario, Hearn could have been charged with insulting the imperial family and thrown into a prison. Therefore, it is safe to conclude that

205   Ebihara. Shinto War Gods of Yasukuni Shrine. ibid.
206   Wikipedia: Yōkai. ibid.

he intentionally omitted the character description of Emperor Antoku, or the Dark Lord, since there was pressure from the totalitarian and emperor-centered Meiji Government.

Other Preternatural Creature in the Medieval Japan

There are many other eerie and entertaining preternatural creatures in medieval Japanese legends other than ghosts of human beings. They are different from Yōkai[207] and Oni[208] who were lost humanity because of their conduct or extreme circumstances during their earthly life. They all transformed into Yōkai or monsterous creatures out of jealousy, grief, sorrow and vengeful thoughts like Hannya in Zeami's Noh theatre and ghosts of Taïra clan warriors in Hearn's Mimi-Nashi-Hoichi. However, many Yōkai and Oni were born preternatural beings with no human past. Some of them were good, but many were evil and harmful to human society. Therefore these evil creatures were eventually slaughtered by well-known illustrious heroes.

Shutendouji

Catrien Ross's study (1996)[209] listed several examples of these mythological creatures in Japanese legends and folklore. For instance, according to *Otogi-zoshi* (御伽草子)[210] the collection of medieval legends, there was an Oni named *Shutendoji* (酒呑童子)[211], whose name literally means "sake-drinking lad". Since his name was coming from his preference to sake, he consumed a large quantity of alcohol according to the legend. He was a brutal character who lived in the

---

207   Wikipedia: Yōkai. ibid.
208   Wikipedia: Oni (folklore). ibid.
209   Ross. ibid.
210   Wikipedia: Otogizōshi. Online at http://en.wikipedia.org/wiki/Otogi_Zoshi
211   Wikipedia: 酒呑童子. http://ja.wikipedia.org/wiki/%E9%85%92%E5%91%91%E7%AB%A5%E5%AD%90

mountains and terrorized people in a small village named Oe (大枝) in today's Kyoto prefecture. He tormented people by robbing villagers and kidnapping women and eating people.

In most versions of the legend, he was born as an Oni and had no human past. However, in some minor versions he was previously human but transformed into Oni. For instance, in a story of Echigo (越後) or present Nigata district, he was an unusually handsome lad, and young and old women alike fell in love with him. However, he broke their hearts by declining advances from all of them. Finally, the furies and wrath of these women transformed him into a dreadful looking creature[212].

He was a very powerful Oni who continued to kidnap and devour humans including children of important government officials. The court and the government officials failed any attempt to track down or stop him because he was clever and elusive. In many different districts in Japan, there are various versions of the story of Shutendoji. In some versions of the story, he and his company practiced a gruesome cannibalism and consumed sake mixed with the blood of beautiful princesses, not only eating their flesh. In most versions he was the head of the Oni band and led them to do robberies, kidnapping and murders instead of acting alone as a type of gang leader.

Finally, the court astrologer Abe no Seimei (921 – 1005)[213] tracked down the location where the monster lived using the power of divination and gave his findings to Emperor Ichijo (986 – 1010). Abe was an onmyōji, a leading specialist

---

212   Wikipedia: 酒呑童子. ibid.
213   Wikipedia: Abe no Seimei (安倍晴明). http://en.wikipedia.org/wiki/Abe_no_Seimei

of onmyōdō who exercised mystical powers during his time. He was responsible for advising on the spiritually correct way and the well-being of emperors and the government. The emperor ordered four Samurai warriors to destroy Shutendoji. However, they were reluctant to go after him out of fear and knew that they were no match with this powerful monster. Then, the emperor dispatched Minamoto no Yorimitsu (948 – 1021)[214] and Fujiwara no Yasumasa, (958 - 1036) a couple of illustrious legendary heroes, to look after Shutendoji.

After praying to Buddha for strength, these warriors learned that Shutendoji liked not only sake and young maidens, but also Yamabushi or mystic seekers. An old man with white hair advised them to change their attires to look like mystics, hiding their armor in their baggage. An old woman who claimed to have been captured by the monster 200 years ago guided them to his hideout. When Shutendoji learned her muscles and bones were extremely hard, he decided to make her his washerwoman instead of human sashimi[215].

Arriving at the hideout, the group of warriors pretended to be lost in the mountains and asked Shutendoji's servants to let them stay overnight. The owner of the house who was already over 200 years old but still looked like a young boy, agreed, and spent all night with them drinking, eating human hotpot and talking about himself and his spoils. After telling a long story about him and entertaining the guests, Shutendoji fell into a drunken slumber. Then, he revealed his true identity as Oni. His true form is generally considered as an ordinary looking Oni with large humanoid body and two horns on his

214   Wikipedia: Minamoto no Yorimitsu (源頼光). http://en.wikipedia.org/wiki/Minamoto_no_Yorimitsu
215   Ross. ibid.

head. Yet, according to some legends, he was a gigantic life form with a great red body, black left foot, white right foot, blue left hand, a yellow right hand, and a huge head with fifteen eyes and five horns. Minamoto no Yorimitsu and other warriors took up their swords and decapitated the monster, but the head did not die and flew up and retaliated on these warriors out of the fury. The monster's teeth sank into helmet of Yorimitsu who gouged out a couple of furious eyes of Shutendoji. The head finally deceased, dropping on the floor motionless and a group of Samurai warriors carried it back to Kyoto and publicly displayed it and eventually placed it in the Byodoin (平等院) temple[216].

Apparently, Shutendoji had a similar physiology to a reptile since his decapitated head did not die right away. When the head of a soft-shell turtle or snake is removed, it can stay alive and conscious for some time due to its low metabolic rate, and some have been known to attack the person who has separated its head from its body. Japan has a long culinary history of consuming soft-shell turtles, so that the writer could have associated the vigorous organism of the monster with reptilian physiology, in which they were well versed.

The super-human reptile like physiology of Shutendoji may also indicate persistent rebellion against the imperial government to the last breath. Although Shutendoji was described as an evil character in the legends, some are sympathetic to him as they identify him with those who were executed in the Heian Period because of the incompliance to the imperial court.

---

216   Ross. ibid.

In Oe in Kyoto prefecture, where he spent his last years until eventually losing his head, Shutendoji is quite a popular figure for tourists. The Oni Exchange Museum houses more than 200 masks of Oni in Japan, and other ogre demonic creatures from around the world. The library adjunct to the museum houses some 4,000 books and documents concerning demons. The roof of the building has about 15 Onigawara (鬼瓦)[217] or ornamental tiles depicting Oni, some dating from the Sixth Century. The underlined concept of these roof tiles is that good Oni will drive off malevolent forces from the house, and they are still used in Japan as good-luck charms. The museum filled with people following construction and today induces more than 200,000 tourists annually to the once-sleepy community[218].

The story that the head of the infamous Oni was placed in the Byodoin temple at the end may indicate that the model of the character was originally a human with a vengeful spirit that requires appeasement. That would be going back to the story from Echigo district in which he was an unusually handsome boy, and many women wooed him but he stayed away from them. It might be possible to interpret that these women indicate court and government officials who tried to persuade him to serve the emperor. However, he didn't want to do anything with being emperor and said an absolute "no" to these proposals and provoked the anger of the imperial authority. Finally, the furies and wrath of the imperial court officials labeled him as an Oni or the enemy of the emperor descended from the Sun-goddess Amaterasu[219]. Heroes

217   Wikipedia: Onigawara. http://en.wikipedia.org/wiki/Onigawara
218   Ross. ibid.
219   Wikipedia: 酒呑童子. ibid.

like Minamoto no Yorimitsu and Fujiwara no Yasumasa are imperial loyalists and elite guards who were teaching lessons to those who do not want to submit to their authority. However, not everyone in Japan from antiquity to now appreciates the Japanese emperor system and several individuals including Taïra-no-Masakado and Ashikaga Yoshimitsu challenged it.

Shutendoji may be a character modeled after one of these two who challenged the court at the expense of his life during the early Heian Period. Throughout the whole recorded history of Japan after the introduction of the writing system, people who challenged the authority of the emperor were almost always labeled as villains or Oni. Because of this, challenging the emperor system or placing any other person to a higher or equal position to him was considered taboo after the Heian Period. During the 19th and 20th century, the government had a policy to intensify this taboo to brainwash the entire nation, so that they might accept the emperor-centered worldview and the State Shinto without any questions. In public school systems, teachers taught pupils that characters like Shutendoji, Taïra-no-Masakado and Ashikaga Yoshimitsu were the worst examples to follow, since they disrespected the emperor. When the imperial Japan was finally defeated in 1945, the Kokutai or emperor-centered cultic community was dismantled by the Allied force and people obtained the freedom of thoughts and speech.

After the Second World War, Go Nagai (b.1945)[220] a famous Japanese manga artist and a prolific author of science fiction, created a good manga character modeled after Shutendoji. The title and the protagonist's name is also

---

220   Wikipedia: Go Nagai (永井豪). http://en.wikipedia.org/wiki/Go_Nagai

Shutendoji (手天童子)[221] with the same pronunciation but different kanji as the historical villain[222]. His character (手天) indicates "heavenly hands" instead of "drinking sake" (酒呑). The Nagai's character does not drink sake like his predecessor, since he is a children's hero. He is an Oni, who lives in three different time settings: medieval age, today's world and future, and fights evil monsters to protect humanity. Nagai described a fascinating fantasy world named *Ongokukai* (鬼獄界) or "the world of Oni" supposedly located in a different universe and dimension. It has a close parallel with the world of Yaksha[223], the prototype of Oni in Buddhist mythology in India. The underlined concept behind this story is the Buddhist worldview from India, China and Japan.

Kintarō

Minamoto no Yorimitsu had a very powerful associate named Sakata no Kintoki when he killed Shutendouji, the terror of the region around Mount Oe. Kintoki is a folk hero from Japanese folklore whose childhood name was Kintarō (金太郎)[224], "Golden Boy". A child of superhuman strength, he was raised by a mountain hag on Mount Ashigara and became friendly with the animals of the mountain. Later, after killing Shutendouji he became a loyal follower of Yorimitsu.

Sakata no Kintoki as a historical person was most likely a mere human without any supernatural power though possessing an extraordinary physical strength and military prowess. However, over years people had developed the legend of Kintaro as a boy with a super-human level of physical

221   Go Nagai. Shutendōji. (Tokyo: Japan: Kadokawa Shoten, 1976/1978)
222   Wikipedia: 手天童子. http://ja.wikipedia.org/wiki/%E6%89%8B%E5%A4%A9%
E7%AB%A5%E5%AD%90
223   Wikipedia: Yaksha. ibid.
224   Wikipedia: Kintarō. http://en.wikipedia.org/wiki/Kintar%C5%8D

strength whose parents are both preternatural creatures. Over years, many creative and imaginative writers developed several competing stories about his parents and upbringing.

According to the most well known story, he grew up in Ashigarayama (足柄山) a mountain in Hakone (箱根) district in today's Kanagawa prefecture. There is a well known song Ashigarayama no Kintarō which is widely sung among Japanese children[225]. In one legend, his mother Yama-uba (山姥) is a powerful female yōkai who lives in the mountains and his father Raijin (雷神), or thunder god, has a close resemblance to Oni. Another legend has it that his father is a red dragon instead of a thunder god. In another, his father is a human named Sakata though his mother is Yama-uba. Yet another story has both of his parents as humans, but he possesses supernatural power since he has a divine inspiration[226]. The locations where he is said to have grown up vary according to various districts.

All versions of the story agree that he grows up in a mountain region and becomes friendly with the animals. Most of his friends are bears, deers, monkeys, and hares living around the mountains. Bears are his best friends and he develops basic military skills by practicing sumo and horse riding with them. His mother is a very kind woman and loves him very much though a yōkai is feared by humans in most versions of the legend. His father is absent and he grows up among animals instead of people. Using his extraordinary physical strength, he helps his mother by cutting trees and

---

225   Ozaki's text is based on a boring version that both of Kintaro's parents are humans. However, the legend in Mount Ashigara tells her mother was a Yama-uba and his father a thunder god.

226   Yei Theodora Ozaki. Japanese Fairy Tales. (shinanootsha. eBook, 1908)

doing farm work. He also enjoys smashing up rocks and stones with bare hands as a favorite pastime[227].

The super-human level of his physical strength amazed his mother and villagers. The legend says that the remarkable thing about this child was his great strength, and as he grew older he grew stronger and stronger, so that by the time he is eight years of age he is able to cut down trees as quickly as the woodcutters.

One day, an old man comes to the village to test Kintaro's physical strength and recruit him as a Samurai if he is as good as the rumors he has heard. He impersonates a woodcutter and asks villagers if he could meet a boy with unusual physical strength. The old Samurai tries Sumo with Kintaro and discovers he is evenly matched with the young boy, though he is a seasoned warrior. The old man says to him, "When you are full-grown you will surely be the strongest man in all Japan." The old man introduces himself not as a woodcutter but a vassal of Minamoto no Yorimitsu and tells his mother, "And you, mother, have you not thought of taking your child to the Capital, and of teaching him to carry a sword as befits a samurai?" Kintaro decides to go to Kyoto to become a great Samurai and to please his mother. His mother is more than confident of his physical strength, sword arts and other combating skills required for a Samurai warrior. However, she is more concerned with his lack of social skills and education in the aristocratic manner necessary for the life in Kyoto due to his wild upbringing in the mountains. However, the old man promises to be responsible in educating the young lad and persuades her to let him go[228].

---

227   Ozaki. ibid.
228   Ozaki. ibid.

When he was about to leave the village for Kyoto, Kintaro promises never to forget his mother, and tells her that as soon as he is a Samurai wearing two swords he would build her a home and take care of her in her old age. When Kintaro leaves the mountain village with the old man, the animals Kintaro tamed come to the foot of the mountain to see him off[229].

Having arrived at Kyoto the old warrior takes Kintaro at once to his Lord, Minamoto no Yorimitsu, and tells him all about Kintaro and how he had found the child. Yorimitsu is delighted with the story, and having commanded Kintaro to be brought to him, immediately makes him one of his vassals. Yorimitsu educates Kintaro in military arts, academics and social manners required in the capital. When the boy grows up to be a man, his master renames him to Sakata no Kintoki and makes him the Chief of Shitennou (四天王), the *four heavenly braves*, since he is the strongest of his soldiers Soon after the event of ascension and installation to the office, Kintoki is ordered to accompany his master Yorimitsu on a mission to defeat Shutendouji, a cannibal monster that strikes people around Kyoto with fear. In the Kintaro legend, Sakata no Kintoki instead of Minamoto no Yorimitsu beheads Shutendouji[230].

After defeating the monster, Kintoki rises to celebrity status as the most powerful warrior and the greatest hero of his country, and great power and honor and wealth comes to him. He now fulfills his promise to his aging mother to build a comfortable home for her, and she lives happily with him in the capital to the end of her days[231]. The legend states that Kintoki

---

229   Ozaki. ibid.
230   Ozaki. ibid.
231   Ozaki. ibid.

defeated many monsters, gangsters and bandits during his life time. He passed at the age of 55 from an unknown disease that seriously elevated his fever. According to the standard of the Heian Period, 55 years of life was considered long enough as a warrior. However, as a person with preternatural parents and super-human attributes, readers must conclude that his life was too short. He died even before his master Minamoto no Yorimitsu who was older and a mere human. He started his life as a super-human "Golden Boy" but died in a very human way[232].

Nue

A nue (鵺)[233] is another mythological preternatural creature found in Japanese legends and folklore. Legends described it as having the head of a monkey, the body of a tanuki or raccoon dog, the legs of a tiger and a snake as a tail. People feared Nue as a creature to bring misfortune and illness. *The Tale of the Heike* (平家物語) says that Emperor Konoe becomes seriously ill after having terrible nightmares every night, and a dark cloud appears at two a.m. on the roof of the imperial palace in Kyoto during the summer of 1153. So a Samurai named Minamoto no Yorimasa stakes out the roof one night and fires an arrow into the cloud, out of which falls a dead nue. The emperor recovers from the illness and gives Yorimasa a powerful sword named Shishiou (獅子王) which means "the Lion King"[234].

Nue was considered a creature with very powerful supernatural power, including the ability to curse and cause

---

232   Wikipedia: 金太郎. http://ja.wikipedia.org/wiki/%E9%87%91%E5%A4%AA%E9%83%8E

233   Wikipedia: Nue. http://en.wikipedia.org/wiki/Nue

234   Wikipedia: 鵺. http://ja.wikipedia.org/wiki/%E9%B5%BA

illnesses and disasters even after death. Therefore, the body
of the creature was carefully buried following the precise
procedure of the Buddhist ceremony, since people feared a
curse. At the same time, each legend has a different ending
regarding the burial of the creature since many imaginative
writers added their own stories to the original legend. During
the Muromachi Period, Zeami Motokiyo, the popular playwright,
also wrote a *Noh* script titled Nue dealing with the events
described in The Tale of the Heike. The story of Nue continues
its expansion and embellishment by several creative writers
and becomes a part of popular entertainment in the pre-
modern and modern era. The creature also appears in many
contemporary anime, manga and video games.

Several Buddhist temples also developed their own
legends that the body of the very same Nue was buried under
their sites, though there was only one corpse. These stories
stirred up public curiosity through the centuries and have
brought in many visitors to these temples. In the modern era,
these visitors have brought in great profits to the temples and
the local communities.

[235] Six warriors who defeated Shutendouji including Sakata no Kintoki & Minamoto no Yorimitsu[236].

---

235   Was available May 2011: http://image.search.yahoo.co.jp/search?ei=UTF-8&fr=top_ga1_sa&p=%E9%85%92%E5%91%91%E7%AB%A5%E5%AD%90

236   The picture is used under "fair dealing" (Canada) and "fair use" (USA) provisions in copyright law.

3

Spirituality & Afterlife Concept in Early-Modern Japan

Japanese modernity started in the mid-Muromachi Period as guns and cannons and other modern weapons and instruments arrived from the Europe. In his masterpiece *Princess Mononoke* (1997)[237], Hayao Miyazaki (b.1941)[238] illustrates this power shift in the growing conflict between the natural world and newly industrialized humans.[239]

Historians describe this period as a time of great upheaval when the relationship between humanity and nature was radically changing in Japan. Modern weapons like "hand-cannons" and other firearms were brought in by the Portuguese in 1543 and the second Iron Age or so called "Iron Age of modernity" was dawning[240]. It was a significant change in technology for Japan that came primarily through the hands of Spanish and Portuguese sailors.

---

237   Wikipedia: Princess Mononoke. Was available March 2011: http://en.wikipedia.org/wiki/Princess_mononoke
238   Wikipedia: Hayao Miyazaki. Was available March 2011: http://en.wikipedia.org/wiki/Hayao_Miyazaki
239   Lucy Wright. Forest Spirits, Giant Insects and World Trees: The Nature Vision of Hayao Miyazaki. Journal of Religion and Popular Culture, 2005.
240   Isao Ebihara. All The World IS Anime. (Dayton, TN: USA: Global Ed Advance, 2010)

The nation's technological modernization from this point, however, was extremely slow until the 19th century, since the Tokugawa shogunate government cut off the diplomatic relationships with Western nations in 1639. As well, in a socio-political sense, Japan remained in the medieval era until the Meiji Restoration in 1868.

Miyazaki's Princess Mononoke vividly describes the negative side of modernity and destructive weapons. Newly introduced firearms from the West increased the destructiveness to both humans and the environment. Remorseless and power hungry warmongers were supported in their manslaughters and mass destructions using these "new toys" purchased from the West.

The later half of the Muromachi Period was also characterized by religious wars and conflicts. During this period, monks in Honganji (本願寺) and other temples in Pure Land schools were becoming more and more aggressive and violent intimidating the authority and general public. They often brainwashed peasants to instigate *ikki* (一揆) or rebellion against authority, promising them a successful rebirth as bodhisattvas by doing so. The authority and power of Ashikaga shogunate sharply declined after the Onin War (大仁の乱) in which *Shugo* or the provincial governors appointed by the shogunate government lost their power[241]. The religiously motivated rebellions happened frequently and Daimyo under the shogun started acting independently from the central authority and became Sengoku Daimyo (戦国大名) or feudal warlords. The entire nation was moving toward complete chaos and lawlessness. Feudal warlords considered this chaotic state

---

241   Blum. ibid.

as a great opportunity to ascend to the ruling power or the whole nation. Many peasants and commoners also considered this an opportunity to ascend to higher positions and decided to serve the warlords and become Samurai warriors, leaving the farm behind. Virtually every male had a chance to seize the entire nation and become a new ruler simply by winning in the battlefield and proving himself a mighty Samurai.

This new feudal era birthed many preternatural legends that reflected the social and technological upheavals fo the day.

Preternatural World During the Feudal Era

InuYasha (犬夜叉)[242], a Feudal Fairy Tale or Sengoku Otogizōshi (戦国御伽草子), is a Japanese anime and manga series written by Rumiko Takahashi (b. 1957)[243] a popular anime and manga artist in Japan. InuYasha the protagonist is a *hanyō* or half-human and half-yōkai creature who is also a very powerful warrior born in the late Muromachi period. Takahashi used the same kanji characters (夜叉) yasha/yaksha in Hindu/Buddhist mythology. According to the story setting, his father is a canine type Yōkai and his mother an aristocratic woman from the imperial court. His combating skills are a good match for Sesshomaru (殺生丸) his older half-brother, who was fully Yōkai and whose characters meant to be a "killer". InuYasha initially wants to use the power of *the Sacred Shikon Jewel* to become a full-blooded Yōkai like Sesshomaru and increase his physical strength and supernatural power.

Meanwhile, after falling in love with the priestess Kikyo, he changes his mind about the jewel. He still wants it, but

242   Wikipedia: InuYasha. http://en.wikipedia.org/wiki/InuYasha
243   Wikipedia: Rumiko Takahashi. http://en.wikipedia.org/wiki/Rumiko_Takahashi

intends to use it to become a human. However, Naraku (奈落) the primary antagonist and evildoer whose kanji characters means Hades in Buddhist mythology, manipulates both of them into believing they had been betrayed by one another. Using his shapeshifting power, Naraku, takes Kikyo's form to draw out and taunt InuYasha, and InuYasha's form to mortally wound Kikyo. Before Kikyo dies, she also shoots the real InuYasha with a sacred arrow to seal him to a sacred tree. After this, he is sealed to the tree for 50 years until Kagome Higurashi, a preteen girl from the modern world finally releases him[244].

Kagome Higurashi is a modern day middle-school student and the reincarnation of the priestess Kikyo whom InuYasha was once in love with. She has a part of the sacred Shikon Jewel unknowingly hidden inside her body. She time-travels to the Sengoku Period (戦国時代) or Warring States period sometime between 15th century and the beginning of the 17th Century. This era overlapped with the late Muromachi Period that is characterized by a time of social upheaval and series of civil wars. When Kagome goes into a well house to retrieve her cat, she discovers that she can travel back and forth between the present and the Sengoku Period through a well at the shrine near her house.

Kagome arrives at the Sengoku Period 50 years after Kikyo's death going through the time-traveling wormhole in the well. When Kagome arrives at the Sengoku Period, the local people hail her as the reincarnation of their village's long-deceased priestess, Kikyo. However, many evil Yōkai come after her since she has a part of the sacred jewel inside her

244   List of InuYasha characters. http://en.wikipedia.org/wiki/List_of_InuYasha_characters

body. Because Kagome needs a partner and bodyguard in her travels, she frees InuYasha who was sealed to a sacred tree by Kikyo. When Kagome first frees InuYasha from Kikyo's spell, his initial thought is to destroy the woman he quickly identifies by smell as his "killer" since she is the reincarnated self of Kikyo. Nevertheless, Kikyo's baby sister, Kaede, now an old woman and the village leader, enables Kagome to control Inu-Yasha with a word *Osuwari* (お座り) which meant "sit" as an owner would say to a dog. After this, the two fight side by side, kill many monsters and protect each other, but the jewel's power proves to be a strong lure for evil Yōkai[245]. While searching for other pieces of the sacred stone and defeating evil monsters together with Kagome, InuYasha discovers he has feelings for her[246].

Sesshomaru, Inu-Yasha's older half-brother is an extremely powerful full-blooded Yōkai, invincible when fighting, and is able to fly in the air. Unlike most other Yōkai he shows no interest in possessing any piece of the Shikon Jewel, since he was feeling confident of his own strength. He finds using of the gem to enhance his power as distasteful. Later, he is emotionally attached to a human female child named Rin, who never shows any fear of Sesshomaru's true Yōkai identity. He later beomes her guardian and protects her at all costs. Naraku learns this and attempts to take advantage of it as a weakness. He tries to manipulate him by abducting and using her as a hostage but fails. Since then, Sesshomaru is disgusted with Naraku and makes destroying the monster his primary goal[247].

245   List of InuYasha characters. ibid.
246   InuyashaWorld. http://www.inuyashaworld.com/
247   List of InuYasha characters. ibid.

Togao (闘牙王) or Inu no Taisho (犬の大将) in the English version, is the father of InuYasha and Sesshomaru. He is a powerful yōkai lord who was once known throughout Japan, but never formally addressed with a name. Togao fathers two sons by two different mothers: Sesshomaru from a canine type Yōkai named Inukimi (犬君), and InuYasha from a human femele named Izayoi (十六夜). Just like Sesshomaru, Togao usually appears in humanoid warrior mode, but his true identity is a ferocious wolf or wild canine with super natural powers[248].

Togao is apparently a Yōken (妖犬) or Yōkai Dog carrying the same motif as Yatsufusa (八房) in *Nansō Satomi Hakkenden* (南総里見八犬伝), written in the late Edo Period. Yatsufusa was an extremely intelligent canine with human-like personality and supernatural attributes that endow his power to Eight Samurai characters posthumously. The Eight Samural warriors are humans and protagonists of the story, but possess supernatural force from the mystical canine. InuYasha and Sesshomaru are sons of the powerful mythological Yōken but in humanoid figures. They could be modeled after warriors from Nansō Satomi Hakkenden who were spiritual children of Yatsufusa[249]. People created stories about extremely intelligent dogs with supernatural powers likely because they lived very closely to canines. Dogs lived close to humans as useful companions throughout millennia as there is enough archeological evidence to show that dogs were the first animals domesticated by early humans.

Naraku is the series' primary antagonist responsible for most of the characters' misfortunes, including the death of Kikyo. He is classified as a Hanyo or half-yōkai and half-human

248   List of InuYasha characters. ibid.
249   物語の犬たち. http://homepage3.nifty.com/purinto/library/inu.html

character just as InuYasha. Nevertheless, unlike other Yōkai characters, Naraku originally comes into existence from the fusion of a full human, crippled bandit named Onigumo and numerous minor Yōkai. Onigumo is also deeply in love with Kikyo, whom he manipulates to fight with InuYasha to death. He has a power to assimilate or incorporate other Yōkai or human individuals into himself and get larger and stronger. He is obsessed with the Shikon Jewel that would make him a full Yōkai and more powerful. Throughout the whole series, he creates many subordinates out of his own body to aid his goal of killing his opponents and obtain the Shikon Jewel that might endorse him with the ultimate power. At the end of the story, Naraku is killed in the final battle with InuYasha, his company and Sesshomaru. At the end, he restores the human soul of Onigumo and dies in peace expressing regret at not being able to have Kikyo for his own. Naraku's peaceful death has a close parallel to Zeami's theatre in which souls of demonic characters are appeased and finally find peace at the end of the play. Just like Zeami's characters Naraku who was formally Onigumo, the bandit had enough reasons to transform into a Yōkai or vengeful spirit[250].

In the InuYasha series, there are many other human and Yōkai characters linked to Japanese myth and folklore. Miroku (弥勒) was a lecherous monk, aged 18, who travels the countryside performing spiritual services such as exorcisms and demon exterminations. Apparently, he is named after *Miroku* (弥勒)[251] a bodhisattva and popular Buddhist deity after the Heian Period appointed to be a future Buddha by the historical Gautama Buddha. Miroku in this story was a carnal

---

250   List of InuYasha characters. ibid.
251   Wikipedia: 弥勒菩薩. ibid.

human quite apart from a deity being trained to reach the Buddha-hood, since he was notorious for his recurring lechery, usually manifesting as shameless flattery, flirtatious conducts and asking every woman he meets to bear him a child. He also deliberately falsifies his spiritual work as a priest to earn comfortable rewards.

Nevertheless, Miroku is capable of exercising supernatural forces. For instance, he can attack monsters with a sacred staff and Buddhist sutra scrolls. He is also able to blow out his enemies with the *Wind Tunnel* embedded in the palm of his right hand. It was originally a hereditary curse inflicted by Naraku upon his grandfather. Miroku first met InuYasha as he was stealing the Shikon Jewel, causing them to combat one another until Kagome intervenes. After Miroku explains his situation, Kagome asks him to join her and InuYasha, to pursue the common goal of defeating Naraku. Over time, Miroku grows up and begins to focus his affections more exclusively on Sango, an attractive female demon slayer, as his personality matures.

Shippo, an orphaned young fox Yōkai, originally attempts to steal the Shikon Jewel from Kagome and InuYasha, wishing to become stronger and to avenge his father's death. After his plan fails, Kagome and InuYasha support him after hearing his story. Later, Shippo becomes their companion for the rest of the series. He normally has a similar appearance to a young human boy except for certain fox-like features such as a long bushy tail and hairy legs and feet. He has shape-shifting power but his other forms do not last long due to his lack of training as a Yōkai[252].

---

252   List of InuYasha characters. ibid.

The character of Shippo was apparently modeled after Inari Ōkami, (稲荷大神) the fox god. The fox god was a popular figure in both Shinto and Buddhist beliefs and many country houses of wealthy families hosted their shrines in it. It was one of the principal deities of both Shinto and Buddhist myths, considered the symbol of worldly success. There is a well known sushi recipe named Inarizushi (稲荷寿司), consisting of a pouch of fried tofu filled with sushi rice that is named after Okami as according to legend he is known as being very fond of aburaage (油揚げ), or fried Tofu[253].

Kirara (雲母) is Nekotata (猫又) or a feline Yōkai originally in Sango's company. She usually remained in the form of a small domestic cat. However, she reveals her identity as a large ferocious cat Yōkai larger than a tiger with the ability to fly. InuYasha and his company often ride on her back when she is in a combating mode. She is an intelligent creature and able to understand human language though she never takes human form in front of InuYasha and his company. In the late Muromachi or Sengoku Period when she meets InuYasha and his friends, Kirara is already over 300 years old[254]. According to the folklore, there are two different forms of Nekomata. The first is born as Yōkai and usually lives in the mountains. People are afraid of them since they are vicious and often eat humans. Many legends of this first type were created after the Kamakura Period[255].

The second form of Nekomata are originally aged domestic cats and mutated into a Yōkai when they were older

253   In today's Japan, udon noodle with fried tofu is called Kitsune udon and soba noodle with the same topping Kitsune soba.

254   犬夜叉の登場人物. http://ja.wikipedia.org/wiki/%E7%8A%AC%E5%A4%9C%E5%8F%89%E3%81%AE%E7%99%BB%E5%A0%B4%E4%BA%BA%E7%89%A9

255   Wikipedia: 猫又. http://ja.wikipedia.org/wiki/%E7%8C%AB%E5%8F%88

than 10. According to some popular legends, these cats can accumulate knowledge and increase wisdom as they grow older. Some also believed that felines are able to understand even human language when they are 7 or older. Depending on the legend, these cats evolved into the Yōkai either during their life time or after death. The legends concerning this kind of Nekotata developed during the Edo Period when common people started customarily owning cats as their pets. They enjoyed imaginative entertaining stories about their pets, and felines were becoming as popular as canines during these days. Felines have been considered as an intelligent and man's best friend from the medieval era in the same way as canines. Just as the legends or creative stories about a Yōken or Yōkai dog, people have developed creative and fanciful stories about a Yōkai cat. Besides Nekotata, there are various Yōkai cats with supernatural power in Japanese ghost stories. Some of them have shape-shifting power and often appear in human form.

From antiquity, felines were considered spiritual animals because of their tremendous physical ability to hunt prey even larger than themselves and mysterious appearance, especially their shiny eyes at night. People of all ages adored and feared felines simultaneously because of their mysterious attributes. In the West, people considered them demons and massacred them. During the medieval period to the early modern era, Japanese also believed that a great curse rested upon anyone who killed cats. However, almost all felines were wiped out from Europe during the same period, and the Black Death pandemic soon followed since rodents multiplied as the consequence. Ironically, this Japanese belief came true in the Europe when millions of people died for the "curse" or the Black Death, partly caused by the lack of cats.

Japanese during the Edo Period also believed that cats with longer tails tended to mutate into Nekotata, since these creatures had split tails. They preferred short tailed cats, because of this association. Some scholars argue that it was the reason that Japanese cats tend to have shorter tails in comparison with those from the rest of the world. There is also a breed of domestic felines named "Japanese Bobtail" with an unusually short tail more closely resembling the tail of a rabbit than that of other cats. Western breeders created the breed from ordinary domestic cats brought into the West from there.

Domestic cats immigrated to Japan around the Seventh Century along with Buddhism and literacy from China. They became useful by hunting rodents and other harmful pest animals. The first felines in Japan had the additional important mission to protect precious documents from rodents. It is therefore understandable that Japanese in the Edo Period created imaginative stories about felines as well as canines.

Introduction of Christianity to Japan

The Portuguese Roman Catholic priest Francis Xavier first introduced Christianity into Japan in 1549. Around that time, quite a few local feudal lords welcomed the missionaries due to economic and military reasons[256]. Some of the Japanese became the first generation of believers in Jesus Christ, often because they were tired of Buddhist temples causing rebellions and violent civil strives over centuries. They wanted to increase their arms by trading with the Portuguese, and attempted to

---

256   Megumi Watanabe. "Modern Diffusion of Christianity in Japan" MA. Thesis, University of Hawaii, HI, 2004.

access Portuguese trading companies through Roman Catholic missionaries. This coincided with the time Hayao Miyazaki describes as the arrival of modern weapons from Europe[257].

For approximately one century, there was a 'honeymoon period' between Christianity and Japanese rulers. However, when Toyotomi Hideyoshi (1537 - 1598) came to the power and stabilized the nation by conquering minor warlords and officially replacing the Ashikaga shogunate. Toyotomi ended the era of "Warring States" by establishing a strong and stable government. He started his military carrier as a lowest rank soldier of Oda Nobunaga (1534 - 1582) since he was not born as a Samurai class person. After the death of his master, he climbed up the ladder to the rulership of the nation. Although his master Oda was in favor of Christianity, Toyotomi was against it. After becoming the ruler, he issued an expulsion order to all of the foreign missionaries and began to persecute Christians. We can speculate several reasons for this. First, he wanted to eliminate the influence of a several rival warlords who had converted to Christianity. Takayama Ukon (1552 - 1615) and Otomo Sorin (1530 - 1587) and several others were known as Christian Daimyo or warlords. Possibly Toyotomi was afraid they might use Christianity to manipulate peasants to rebel against his government in the same way the Buddhist monks did over the centuries.

Another possible reason that Toyotomi Hideyoshi persecuted Christianity was its denial of the class system. Christianity holds to the position that all humans are equal under one and only creator God. However, in the medieval and early modern Japan had a caste system similar to that of India

---

257   Wikipedia: Hayao Miyazaki. ibid.

in which the emperor and his relatives are the top, the Samurai class the second and all others are the lowest. During the Sengoku Period the classes were reclassified because there were many social upheavals and some like Toyotomi climbed up the ladder from the bottom to the top. However, he found that, whenever society was stabilized, the class system must be re-established. He was afraid that another ambitious person like him from the peasant class might challenge his regime and defeat it. Toyotomi found Christianity as an ideological obstacle to re-establish the class system after the Warring States period.

Toyotomi regime was defeated by Tokugawa family after the death of Hideyoshi, the founder of the oligarchy. Tokugawa Ieyasu (1543 – 1616), the head of the Tokugawa clan defeated Toyotomi Hideyori the son of Hideyoshi, and started a new shogunate government. Ieyasu and his descendents persecuted Christians even more harshly than the Toyotomi regime. When Tokugawa Iemitsu (1604 – 1651), the grandson of Ieyasu, was the Shogun, a series of failed rebellions arose against Iemitsu's anti-Christian policies in today's Kyushu district. In 1637 nearly all Japanese Christians were annihilated after an armed revolt in a small community named Shimabara in Kyushu. Thousands were killed in the battle during the revolt and countless more were executed afterwards[258].

After that, Christianity was outlawed, and all believers were executed unless they recanted their faith. Megumi Watanabe (2004) noted that the Tokugawa shogunate introduced *Fumie* (踏み絵) as an effective method to prove

---

[258]   Wikipedia: Tokugawa Iemitsu. http://en.wikipedia.org/wiki/Tokugawa_Iemitsu

whether the person was a Christian or not. By this method, a government official ordered a suspect to step on a Christian icon in order to show that a person was not a Christian. If he or she refused it, this person was automatically considered to be a Christian so was imprisoned and executed. During the Edo Period, Japan had two centuries of national seclusion from 1639 to 1854 in order to keep the nation away from Christian influence until US Admiral Matthew Perry (1794-1858) demanded that Japan open its doors to the world. For nearly two centuries, Japan kept their ports closed to all but Dutch and Chinese merchants. Spanish and Portuguese diplomats and missionary activities were totally banned during this period[259].

According to Ohashi (1996), the persecution that triggered the Shmabara Rebellion had a little different nature from previous ones by the Toyotomi and Tokugawa regimes. On this occasion, the shogunate government focused on the peasant class Christians rapidly increasing in the Shimabara region, while previously the authority had targeted the Samurai class believers[260]. During Iemitsu's reign the Tokugawa shogunate increased the belief that the Christianity was going to permeate the commoners' class and become a great threat to the rulers. Ohashi maintains that the Shimabara Rebellion stands as a turning point, making qualitative change in the Christian prohibition from the *bateran* or Samurai class believers to the wider Christian population. Toyotomi Hideyoshi and first two Tokugawa Shoguns did not care about the Christian belief among commoners and peasants, since they were of

---

259   Watanabe. Ibid.
260   Yukihiro Ohashi. New Perspectives on the early Tokugawa Persecution. Japan and Christianity (London: UK. Macmillan Press LTD, 1996), 46-62

little influence to the entire society. However, they increased in number and became more influential during Iemitsu's period, so that the shogunate government was compelled to take action. Concerning the different nature of Shimabara's persecution from the previous ones, Ohashi contends:

> What is important to note, in conclusion, is that the Shimabara Rebellion marks a turning point in the nature of the Christian suppression: the focus of government attention shifts demonstrably now from the *bateran* — which we have seen meant missionaries and Christians of the warrior class — to the general populace. At the same time, we have suggested that the enforcement of the persecution — at least in the Shimabara and Amakusa areas — was an important contributory factory in achieving the complete separation of the military and peasant classes. From the Shimabara Rebellion onwards, it was the Christian populace and the threat of rebellion that they posed which, to the *Bakufu* authorities, became the greatest Christian threat.

Ohashi maintains that before the rebellion happened in Shimabara, the Tokugawa shogunate government was relatively lenient to the bateran or Samurai class Christians, although they strongly discouraged Christian faith among warriors and took away many privileges from believers. But the Tokugawa shogunate made new efforts to tighten controls on the Christian populace[261]. The rebellion led by the peasant class believers was a new threat to the regime and must be terminated. Christians in Japan had to face more serious and ruthless persecution and all foreign missionaries were expelled from the country. All believers in the Shimabara district were arrested and executed, unless they gave up their faith.

---

261   Yukihiro Ohashi. ibid.

It is generally agreed that the Tokugawa shogunate was afraid of colonization by Spain with its much more advanced technology and powerful military and that the Spanish government might use Christianity as a convenient tool to colonize Japan. Because of this, Tokugawa Iemitsu enacted the foreign relations policy named Sakoku (鎖国) meaning "locked country" around the time of Shimabara Rebellion. Under Sakoku no foreigner could enter or any Japanese leave the country on penalty of death. After the policy was enacted, the government closed all ports in the country and terminated diplomatic relationships with most Western nations after expelling the missionaries. However, the shogunate government retained diplomatic relationship with the Netherlands during the era of the "locked country" since she was a Protestant nation with no linkage to the Roman Catholic organization.

The policy remained in effect until 1853 with the arrival of Commodore [262]Matthew Perry (1794 – 1858)[263]. In 1852, Perry embarked on his mission to sail from Norfolk, Virginia for Japan in search of a Japanese trade treaty. Aboard a steam frigate, he was met by representatives of the Tokugawa shogunate and told to proceed to Nagasaki, the only Japanese port open to foreigners at that time.

Perry refused to comply with demands to leave for Nagasaki and ordered his ships to steam past Japanese lines towards the capital of Edo, and point their guns towards the town of Uraga. He then demanded permission to present a letter from President Millard Fillmore (1800-1874), and threatened to use arms if the Japanese boats around the

262   Wikipedia: Sakoku. http://en.wikipedia.org/wiki/Sakoku
263   Wikipedia: http://en.wikipedia.org/wiki/Matthew_C._Perry

American fleet did not disperse. After the Japanese agreed to receive the letter from the American President, Perry landed at Kurihama on July 14, 1853, presented the letter to delegates of the shogunate government and left, promising to return for a reply.

The shogunate authority could also have equated the Shimabara Rebellion the Buddhist rebellions in the previous era that involved the peasant class. So they wanted to eradicate the root of all potential peasant rebellions, since Buddhist led riots during the Muromachi Period weakened and eventually terminated the Ashikaga shogunate. The authority was afraid the pent up energy of discontent among the peasants might take the form of Christian rebellions in the same way as it took the form of Buddhist riots. The Tokugawa shogunate was known for its effectiveness in suppressing its opponents and potential rebels and its ruthlessness to traitors or those who were disloyal to Shogun. They did not the repeat the mistakes of their predesessors that allowed a series of rebellions to weaken the regime. Tokugawa also did not forget to reward those who were loyal to the shogunate government and made significant contributions, so that they maintained their strength for almost 250 years.

Some analysts maintain that the Edo Period under Tokugawa shogunate was a relatively peaceful period in Japan's history. Their technological advancement was delayed greatly since Tokugawa minimized contact with the Western nations. Although the technology was very backward, commoners in big cities accumulated wealth and the non-technological domain of the civilization almost paralleled the West. For example, the restaurant industry boomed during this period in the city of Edo in the same way as many big cities in the Western nations.

Amakusa Shirō Tokisada

The Shmabara Rebellion was led by a teenage leader named Amakusa Shirō (1621 - 1638) also known as Amakusa Shirō Tokisada. According to the legend, he was a Christian Samurai who had an early death due to his faith in Christ. Nevertheless, his upbringing and most of his life before the rebellion remain in mystery. In some legends, he is an illegitimate grandson of Toyotomi Hideyoshi. After the rebellion fails, Amakusa was executed in the aftermath of the fall. His head was displayed on a pike in Nagasaki for a very long time afterward until the flesh was rotten and falling from the skull as a warning to any other potential Christian rebels[264].

In popular culture, Amakusa Shiro is often cast as a tragic villain or demonic character that rejected the salvation of Jesus Christ at the moment of his death or posthumously as a ghost. After becoming a Yōkai, he returned to Earth to destroy the Tokugawa shogunate who put him to death with some of Japan's greatest heroes and villains of the age who were also resurrected as demons. Amakusa Shiro as a vengeful demon is depicted in various literature, movies, anime, manga and video games. Such portrayal includes the novel and movie Makai Tensho (魔界転生)[265], the anime series Rurouni Kenshin, and the Samurai Shodown video game series[266].

These stories in the contemporary pop-culture showing a heroic Christian martyr transformed into a vengeful Yōkai

264   Wikipedia: Amakusa Shirō. http://en.wikipedia.org/wiki/Amakusa_Shiro
265   Futaro Yamada. Makai Tensho. (Tokyo: Kodansha, 1999)
266   Wikipedia: Amakusa Shirō. ibid.

giving away his faith and salvation could be shocking and offensive to many devout Christians. It might indicate that among the majority of Japanese, the theme of vengeance found in Zeami's Noh, and Kabuki is much more popular and persuasive than the forgiveness of enemies taught in the Bible, even in the 21st century. The Bible states, "Vengeance is mine, I will repay, says the Lord," as well as "if your enemy is hungry, feed him; if he is thirsty, give him something to drink; for by so doing you will heap burning coals on his head. Do not be overcome by evil, but overcome evil with good." In a cultural soil in which even a Christian martyr transformed into a vengeful spirit, the teaching of forgiveness is extremely foreign and incomprehensible[267]. Parhaps, Japan's general public is adamant in support of the death sentence despite the relentless urge from the *United Nation* and *Amnesty International* to terminate it, due to the nation's unique tradition to condone vengeance and praise the action of *47 Samurai of Ako* who brutally decapitated the nemeses *Kira Kōzuke no suke* in vengeance for their late master Asano *Takumi no Kami*.

Hiroshi Motomura's (b. 1977) persisted in pursuit of a death sentence for Takayuki Otsuki (b. 1982) who murdered his wife and daughters in 1999. This is an example that Japanese still praise vengeance today. It also has a close parallel to Amakusa Shiro in the movie Makai Tensho and 47 Samurai of Ako. Otsuki brutally murdered Motomura's wife Yayoi, and the couple's 11 month old daughter, Yuka, at their home in Hikari, Yamaguchi Prefecture, in April 1999. According to the Hiroshima High Court ruling in April 2008,

---

267   Romans 12:19–21

Otsuki strangled the three of them to death after an attempt to rape Yayoi. He also committed necrophilia with her body and stole her purse before leaving the Motomura residence. The court initially gave Otsuki a life sentence although prosecutors sought a death sentence, since he was barely 18 at the time of the crime. The crown appealed twice since Motomura fiercely attacked lighter sentences that the judges gave him. Motomura continued a campaign against lesser sentences than the death penalty, and also made a statement to the media that he would wait for Otsuki's release and kill him. A high court finally gave the defendant the death penalty in 2008 and the sentence was finalized in 2012 when the top court rejected Otsuki's appeal[268].

In a press conference at the court when the sentence was finalized, Motomura said that he felt neither pleasant nor happy to hear the decision, though he was satisfied with the sentence against the defendant[269]. This is evidence that one can obtain neither comfort nor peace by punishing a perpetrator. In fact, vengeance only harms the soul instead of the perpetrator and he will not receive an untimate peace unless he accepts the grace of the universal saviour and releases his anger against the man who committed a heinous crime. He was once furious that Otsuki and his attorneys employed a ridiculous defence strategy by saying that he had sex with the Yayoi's body to resuscitate her following a method written in the novel Makai Tensho. Ironically, Motomura himself could be said to have been acting like a ghost of Amakusa

---

268   Motomura: No 'winner' in crime / Supreme Court upholds death sentence in 1999 double murder case. Daily Yomiuri Online, 2012. Online at http://www.yomiuri.co.jp/dy/national/T120221005623.htm.

269   Daily Yomiuri Online. Ibid

Shiro, the main character of the story throughout the whole process of court battle.

On the other hand, in 2006, Charles Carl Roberts walked into an Amish school house in Pennsylvania and slaughtered five schoolgirls before shooting himself. In contrast to Motomura, the survivors of the victims in the Amish community made it clear that they held no malice toward the perpetrator and pursued reconciliation with his family. Gary Chapman (2008) noted that forgiveness was a very large part of this community's attitude and it didn't question whether or not to extend justice or mercy to a killer[270].

---

270   Gary Chapman. Love as a way of life. (Colorado Springs, CO: USA: WaterBook Press, 2008)

[271] Amakusa Shirō Tokisada [272].

---

271   Was available July 2011: http://morinokajiya1929.cocolog-nifty.com/blog/2009/09/no205-15ed.html
272   The picture is used under "fair dealing" (Canada) and "fair use" (USA) provisions in copyright law.

4

Japanese Spirituality in Modern & Contemporary Era

During the Meiji period (1868 through July 1912), the Japanese imperial government systematized traditional Shinto teachings and rites as 'State Shinto' and used it to legitimize the imperial regime and secure the people's loyalty to the emperor. The emperor was regarded as the living god who was a descendant of the great Sun Goddess *Amaterasu*; therefore dying for the emperor was a glorified act pertaining to the greatest honor for the Japanese. This State Shinto, which was closely associated with the emperor system and militarism, had a clear distinction from the primordial Shinto, or primitive and more benign counterpart.

Meiji Restoration & State Shinto

In order to promote the emperor-centred values of loyalty and filial piety on a nation wide scale, the government stipulated in an 1889 constitution that the emperor's sacredness, inviolability, and the unbroken continuity of his divine lineages from antiquity. Within the newly developed imperial cult by the Meiji Government, *Yasukuni Shrine* and

Grand Shrine of Ise assumed the role of contributor to the psychological appeal of the Emperor's divinity.

Yasukuni Shrine was originally built to pacify the souls of Japan's war dead. However, the shrine was gradually shifting to establish the foundation of the militaristic ideology of the Meiji Government and newly developed Emperor Cult. After the Meiji Restoration, Yasukuni was gradually transformed into a centre to impose Kokutai or State Supported Emperor Cult to the Japanese public. The State Shinto was ultimately dismantled by the authority of the Allied Force who controlled the nation during an era of occupation immediately following the Second World War. At this time, the emperor's semi-divine status was denied and he was officially separated from the Shinto religion and declared fully human under the government of Prime Minister Shigeru Yoshida[273].

After the Second World War, 14 convicted [274]Class-A war criminals ("crimes against peace") were enshrined there as gods along with Japanese soldiers who died in the war. After the war, Yasukuni Shrine has been the centre of controversies among the international community primarily because these individuals committed war crimes but were enshrined there as gods as part of the practice of Emperor Worship of the past. But for the majority who opposed the official visit of a prime minister, the main reason for opposition was the enshrinement of the 14 war criminals instead of the Emperor Worship. By the beginning of the 21st century, Emperor Worship was a relic of the past for the majority of Japanese.

---

273   Ebihara. Shinto War Gods of Yasukuni Shrine. ibid.
274   A crime against peace, in international law, referred to the act of military invasion as a war crime, specifically referring to starting or waging war against the integrity, independence, or sovereignty of a territory or state, or else a military violation of relevant international treaties, agreements or legally binding assurances.

Although the emperor system continues to exist today as a symbol of the state, most Yasukuni critics either in Japan or her neighbours do not feel immediate danger. The enshrinement of 14 convicted Class-A war criminals, however, almost instantaneously provoked anger among those who still remember the ugliness of the Pacific War started by Japanese leaders enshrined as *Kami*[275].

For nearly a decade after the early 2000's, many Shinto scholars and politicians have debated about the possibility of separating the enshrinement of these 14 individuals along with the construction of a new facility without Shinto religiosity, to commemorate war dead. However, quite a few Shinto specialists were negative about it since the process of deification is irreversible in Shinto. Some of them even suggested that there would be a curse which might cause undesirable incidents or natural disasters if names of those individuals were removed from the shrine. Some others have suggested that they should pursue an option to transfer these souls to different shrines as deities, if the process of deification was irreversible.

[276]According to Shinto philosophy, once a soul is deified or has become *Kami*, there is no way to reverse the process and make him or her soul ordinary again, since the deification is a supernatural phenomenon beyond the control of human beings. Therefore, there was no way to remove the convicted Class-A war criminals from the list of Kami in Yasukuni Shrine. However, a few Shinto experts and politicians suggested that

275   Ebihara. Shinto War Gods of Yasukuni Shrine. ibid.
276   Kiso kara wakaru Yasukuni Jinja mondai: Bunshi wa dekiru no. Yomiuri Shinbun. June, 2005. Online at http://www.yomiuri.co.jp/feature/fe6700/fe_ya_05060903.htm

[277]Yasukuni could make a separate enshrinement of convicted Class-A war criminals in a different shrine and remove them from Yasukuni, although the process of enshrinement is considered irreversible. These experts insisted that once deified, *Kami* could be moved to a different shrine, stating that enshrinement per se was reversible but the process of deification was irreversible. By doing so, the souls of the Class-A war criminals could be removed, so that the prime minister, emperor or anyone else could visit Yasukuni and pay respect to the soldiers who sacrificed their lives for the country. However, according to other Shinto experts, it is still impossible to transfer Kami to other shrines since any living humans do not possess power and authority to do it, since they are much mightier being than humans.

[278]When Prime Minister Koizumi inquired about the possibility of separate enshrinement of Class-A war criminals at Yasukuni Shrine, the *Association of Shinto Shrines* answered it was unlikely that Yasukuni could do this in the view of basic Shinto principles. Although many individuals from various organizations have suggested removing souls of these individuals from the shrine, Yasukuni officials have been adamant in not making any change.

Although some Shinto believers considered that *Kami* were transferable to other shrines, Yasukuni authorities consistently held the position that it was impossible to do so. The irreversible process of deification in the Shinto religion was reflected in the late 1990's Hollywood popular TV movies

277   Yasukuni's shadow on summit. The Japan Times Weekly. 2004. Online at http://www.japantimes.com/shukan-st/jteds/ed20041210.htm

278   Koizumi distances himself from Shinto view on war criminals. Kyodo News International. 2005. Online at http://www.findarticles.com/p/articles/mi_m0WDQ/is_2005_June_13/ai_n13831368

[279]*Xena the Warrior Princess* (1995-2000) and *Hercules: The Legendary Journeys* (1995-1999). These showed that anyone who ate a substance or divine food named *Ambrosia* or a *golden apple* was deified, or became an invincible god with the power beyond human control and the process of deification was irreversible. According to the story created by Hollywood writers, *Ambrosia* had the power to transform humans into gods no matter what kind of characters they had. Deified gods could be good or evil, wise or foolish.

Although the Hollywood movies were describing the mythological world of ancient Greece, the idea of deification of living beings was similar to Shinto, since the deification of humans and animals was impossible in the world of Greek mythology. Also, though the story was based on the Greek mythology, the divine characters in the movie are often as frail and vulnerable as Shinto Kami than the more robust and invincible deities of original characters in the myth. Many of them are similar to *Izanami*, whose genitals are burned in giving birth to Kagu-Tsuchi the Fire God, and who dies and goes to the netherworld of the *Land of Yomi* to decompose and then is transformed into an evil deity. Even Zeus, the most powerful and ruthless champion of gods, has lost his power as he encounters the conspiracy of [280]*Hera*, his wicked and jealous wife. In the animated version of the same series, he is even more vulnerable and made into a completely powerless mouse by his angry wife. At the same time, Hera the angry wife

---

279   The movie's time and geographic setting was ancient Greece and Ambrosia was food for Greek gods. However, the idea that anyone who ate Ambrosia being deified, was not coming from Greek mythology. It was safe to conclude that the idea was probably stemmed from Shinto or some other Asian myths.
280   Wikipedia: Hera. Online at http://en.wikipedia.org/wiki/Hera

of Zeus is a more wicked character than the one in the original story.

In the myth or the original story, Hera does not exhibit her evil nature as much as the one in the movie, except she fiercely attacks Hercules as her nemesis. At the end she was reconciled with Hercules although she hated him intensely over an extremely long period. On the other hand, in the Hollywood movie, there is no room for reconciliation between the two, and Hera is eventually thrown into a black abyss by Hercules where there was no way out. It is the same abyss where Titans were sealed by their nephew Zeus as he became the ruler of gods. In the movie, Hera is the evil and vengeful wife of Zeus similar to Izanami after she descends to the *Land of Yomi* and eats food there. Because of this, one could speculate that the Hollywood screenwriters were largely influenced by Shinto mythology and adapted some of their components.

In the movie about Hercules and Xena, *Ambrosia* or a *golden apple* was in the hands of gods and usually unobtainable among humans. Anyone who manages to obtain it is extremely fortunate. In the movie, one of recipients is [281]*Callisto*, an extremely complex and enigmatic character featured as a recurring villainess and the nemesis of Xena, born out the protagonist's dark past. Before Xena reforms, she is responsible for the death of Callisto's family when she has her army anihilate the whole village that Callisto was born. Callisto, a child at the time, is traumatized by the attack and goes insane and eventually becomes obsessed with revenge against Xena. The primary purpose for which she obtains the

281   Wikipedia: Callisto (Xena). Online at http://en.wikipedia.org/wiki/Callisto_(Xena)

fruit is to become a powerful deity in order to utterly destroy her nemesis and make her pay the price of what she had done.

However, in Yasukuni, dead soldiers and convicted war criminals are able to obtain a *golden apple* or Ambrosia as the elixir for immortality much easier than Callisto. Officials of Yasukuni Shrine seem to own a factory to manufacture this convenient substance and to use it at any time. In fact, Yasukuni Shrine is a factory of evil gods and a literal [282]Gate of Hades or an evil site like Caesarea Philippi through which souls of Imperial soldiers were walking to the underworld, Hades, Hell Dimension or Land of Yomi.

The metaphor could be made that using the same kind of *Ambrosia* as the one depicted in Hollywood popular entertainment, the Yasukuni officials produce demonic gods out of evil souls when in 1978 they deified the convicted Class-A war criminals. They believed they had summoned back Hideki Tojo (1884–1948), Kiichiro Hiranuma (1867–1952) and all others from the Hades and fed them *Ambrosia,* the divine food. The *deification* of criminals could be said to be *defacation* against peace and humanity.

Oomoto-kyo & Aikido

Oomoto-kyo (大本教) is a significant new Japanese religion that originated from Shinto during the Meiji Period. The religious body was founded in 1892 by Nao Deguchi (1836-1918). She was a housewife from a small city named Fukuchiyama (福知山) in Kyoto Prefecture. She was poverty-stricken and spent all of her possessions to feed her children and physically disabled husband. She declared that she had a "spirit dream" at the lunar New Year of 1892, becoming

---

282   Matthew 16:13-20

possessed by a Shinto Kami named Ushitora no Konjin (未申
の金神) or "golden god of tiger cow". Since then, she became
a faith healer using spiritual power from Shinto deities and
started the new religious organization.

Onisaburō Deguchi (1871–1948) Nao's son in law
became the second guru and was considered an important
figure in Omoto next to his mother in law[283]. When Nao
Deguchi was summoned by the deity Ushitora no Konjin
and started a new religion, it was a small group consisting
of her family, relatives and friends without official capacity.
However, Onisaburō established Oomoto-kyo as a larger
religious organization after taking over the leadership from
his mother in law. Like Nao, Onisaburō was also born into a
poor peasant class family and experienced poverty. However,
he was able to systematize the doctrine and philosophy of
Oomoto-kyo since he was well educated for a man of his
social status. He developed his own unique philosophy of the
universal love coming from the cosmic spirit having integrated
traditional Japanese Shinto, Buddhism traditions and
Western spiritualism. After being officially appointed as Nao's
successor, he pursued training from a government accredited
religious institution and obtained credentials as a Shinto priest.

Nao kept a discreet distance from the State Shinto
because she didn't want to have anything to do with them.
She valued traditional Japanese spirituality and was not ready
to accept a "fake religion" under Western influence that the
government created. However, Onisaburō took more a realistic
stance and posed an appearance to compromise with the
government policy to synthesize all religions with the State

---

283   Wikipedia: Oomoto. Online at http://en.wikipedia.org/wiki/Oomoto

Shinto and enforce emperor worship. He did it to protect the
organization from persecution from the government. Nao and
Onisaburō had a disagreement over this issue for decades
until her death in 1918. There was a time the organization
was named Kōdō Ōmoto (皇道大本) or "Omoto Imperial
Way" reflecting Onisaburō's embracement of State Shinto.
Nevertheless, Onisaburō faced a persecution from the imperial
government, since some of his teachings are contradictory with
the State Shinto and he covertly criticized the divine lineage
of the imperial family. His teaching of universal love based on
the cosmic spirit was contradictory with the State Shinto that
was based on strict nationalism. He was a cosmopolitan with
a belief that sovereign nations would dissolve sooner or later
when human civilization and spiritual culture reached the
state of maturation. The police intervened and destroyed the
headquarters of the organization in 1935. After the Second
World War, Oomoto-kyo was reinstated and registered in
1946 under the Religious Corporations Ordinance by a new
democratic government.

The original spiritual leaders of this movement have
been predominantly women. While Onisaburo Deguchi had
the leadership of the organization, his wife Sumi was the
ceremonial head of the group. The leadership of Oomoto-kyo
has also been hereditary and the movement is guided by its
fifth leader, Kurenai Deguchi a woman from Deguchi family
since 2001. Oomoto-kyo is non-proselytizing, unlike many
other new religions in the Meiji Period, and pursues its goal of
world peace through active participation in the international
ecumenical movement. Today, Oomoto-kyo is a relatively small
religious organization with large worship and administrative

facilities in Ayabe (綾部) and Kameoka (亀岡). They have
several major festivals in Ayabe that attracts thousands of
members from all over Japan. The organization places a great
emphasis on preserving the traditional Japanese arts such as
the tea ceremony, Aikido, Kendo, Noh drama, ceramics, and
calligraphy[284].

Oomoto-kyo is also known as the spiritual foundation
of Aikido (合気道)[285]. Onisaburō was the spiritual mentor of
Morihei Ueshiba (1883-1969) who developed Aikido as a new
martial art in which he synthesized martial studies, philosophy,
and religious beliefs in the Meiji Period. Onisaburō met young
Ueshiba in Mongolia who had completed his training in Judo
in Kodokan (講道館) under Kanō Jigorō (1860–1938) and
a few different schools of Jujutsu and other martial arts.
Unlike most other martial arts practitioners, Ueshiba was
deeply interested in the spiritual world even as a boy. As a
man, he had a great ambition to start a new school of martial
arts integrating Jujutsu and Judo skills, Shinto and Buddhist
spirituality and philosophy. Ueshiba as a young man met
Onisaburō Deguchi in Ayabe after leaving Hokkaidō where he
lived for several years. He was greatly inspired by Onisaburō's
encyclopedic knowledge, charismatic personality and teaching
with elements of both Shinto and Mahayana Buddhism.
The encounter with this rare and amazing teacher with
extraordinary spiritual attributes was of crucial impact on his
personal life and martial art practices later in life.

Later, Ueshiba developed Aikido as a new school of
martial arts through the synthesis of the older martial arts

---

284   Emily Groszos Ooms. Women and Millenarian Protest in Meiji Japan. (Ithaca, NY:
USA. Cornell University Press, 1993)
285   Wikipedia: Aikido. http://en.wikipedia.org/wiki/Aikido

that he had studied and spiritual practices of Oomoto-kyo and traditional Shinto and Buddhism[286]. He tried to integrate the combating skills of the martial arts and religious practices to control supernatural forces like the shamanic warriors of antiquity. According to the theses of Sandra Marie Olliges, Aikido is not simply a martial art or a sport but also a spiritual practice, incorporating Shinto, Zen and Shingon Buddhist, and Omotokyo insights, although not considered a religion. The name Aikido (合気道) combines the kanji for *ai* (合), *ki* (気), and *do* (道), the meaning of Aikido is the Way or spiritual practice of joining, merging, or uniting with spirit or the vital energy of life[287].

Olliges' study also indicates that Morihei Ueshiba's spiritual pilgrimage and search for the meaning of life started early in life. She quoted Kisshomaru Uyeshiba (1969), his son who maintained that Morihei had a deep interest in spirituality even in his childhood[288]. Morihei's parents were supportive and understanding of his spiritual journey, and allowed him to study Shingon Buddhism at age seven and Zen Buddhism at age ten. Shingon is the esoteric or tantric school of Buddhism in Japan, with many similarities to Tibetan Buddhism. Originating in India, it was brought to Japan from China in the early Ninth Century. The ultimate goal of Shingon Buddhism is, having abandoned the identity as a separate self, becoming one with the cosmic Buddha known as *Dharmadhatu*. Shingon teaches that the merger with the organic whole that comprises the entire universe is the highest stage of spiritual development.

---

286   Wikipedia: Aikido. ibid.
287   Sandra Marie Ollinges." A phenomenological study of the experience of cultivating love for all beings in the practice of Aikido" MA. Thesis, Saybrook Graduate School and Research Center, CA, 2008.
288   Kisshomaru Ueshiba. Aikido (Tokyo: Hozansha Publishing, 1969)

The esoteric and mystical part of Aikido could be stemmed from Shingon which seeks out the transcendental and mystic union with bodhisattva and other spiritual beings. Following the tantric practice of Shingon, an Aikido practitioner reads the mind and maneuvers of his or her opponent intuitively[289].

As an avid learner, Morihei was also steeped in Buddhism, Shinto, and many other spiritual practices including Oomoto-kyo later in his life, which contains elements of both Shinto and Mahayana Buddhism. Zen has a more rational and cognitive side of transcendental practice of Buddhism than Shingon and seeks for a solid and stable mental condition in all circumstances. Zen practitioners also seek for *satori* (悟り), or the enlightenment through a long and intense meditation under a harsh environment. Morihei considered Zen practice to seek out for the ultimately stable mental condition and satori or enlightenment as very beneficial for warriors. He also incorporated the concept of universal love based on the cosmic spirit from Oomoto-kyo into his martial art practice as he encountered Onisaburō Deguchi. Later, this Proto New Age like philosophy inherited from his spiritual mentor drew attention in the Western world and brought thousands of non-Japanese into the world of Aikido[290].

Morihei Ueshiba defined Aikido as a very unique martial art based on the principles of harmony, nonviolence, and love for all beings. The Aikido practitioner views himself or herself as part of an interconnected whole, rather than viewing oneself as a separate entity. Aikido has a typically Asian philosophical assumption that one is interconnected with all beings in that one breathes the same air, drinks the same water, and

289   Ollinges. ibid.
290   Ollinges. ibid.

depends on the same Earth for our life. It is based on a different assumption from the traditional Western philosophy in which each life form is a separate entity from each other. Ueshiba's philosophy was very fascinating to many foreigners particularly from the West and so disseminated around the globe quickly. Following a typical Shinto worldview, Ueshiba also viewed that the spiritual world and the material world are not separate, but only different forms of the same reality, each influencing the other[291].

The idea that a person loses identity as a separate individual merging into some other entity as in the philosophy of Aikido is quite foreign to the Western mindset. It is interesting to compare robotic life forms in the American movie *Transformers: Dark of the Moon* (2011) and similar creatures in Japanese real-time Sentai series known as Power Rangers and many other anime and manga stories. The movie technology and morphological characteristics of characters are no doubt modeled after Japanese robotic characters. "Transformers" are also living organisms instead of simply machines just like most robotic creatures called zords in Power Ranger series. According to the storyline, they are intelligent beings came to earth to save the humanity from alien invaders. There are also evil transformers in the same way as Power Rangers have evil robotic creatures. At the end, there is a final and fierce battle between good transformers and bad transformers and the good ones win following the principle that justice always wins.

Nevertheless, there is a crucial difference between underlying philosophical assumptions. In Transformers, each

---

291   Ollinges. ibid.

creature and human acts as a separate entity, while in Power Rangers, characters often merge together and become one entity losing a sense of individuality. For instance, some Transformers take forms of vehicles or airplanes in which humans are allowed to drive or fly. However, whenever they return to their original robotic forms, people who acted as drivers or pilots must come out of the driver's seats or cockpits. People fight the evil doers side by side with Transformers while retaining their separate identity and never become their brains or any other body parts. On the other hand, in Power Rangers and other Japanese shows, people become part of robotic creatures. In Power Rangers, five or six zords become one entity called *Megazord* while their pilots are still inside and ultimately defeat their enemies. In *Neon Genesis Evangelion* (1995), the consciousness of humans and creatures are merged and become one as in the philosophy of Aikido.

Just as Omotokyo, there was a period in which Aikido was forced to embrace State Shinto and fanatic nationalism by the imperial government prior to the Second World War. However, after the war, the organization safely discarded the influence of the Meiji Restorationists and imperial fascism. Before the end of the war, Ueshiba frequently used the term Kokoku-nomichi (皇國ノ道) or "emperor's state's way" and Kodo-seishin (皇道 精神). However, Ueshiba and his organization never used these terminologies after the war, according to the study of Ryuta Kudo and Fumiaki Shishida (2010)[292].

---

292   Ryuta Kudo and Fumiaki Shishida. " Aikido ni okeru Aiki no imi (Meaning of Aiki in Aikido)" MA. Phys. Educ. Hlth. Sport Sci. 55: 453-469. Tokyo, 2010.

Yanagita's Folkloristics & Yōkai Stories

Kunio Yanagita (1875 - 1962), a well known scholar on Japanese folkloristics, made a very significant indepth study of the Yōkai world. Yanagita studied extensively various Yōkai characters in Japanese history as he was convinced that preternatural creatures like Yōkai are an extremely important part of Japanese culture. His study includes Sunakake Babaa, Konaki Jijii, Ittan Momen and many canine and feline type Yōkai characters in Japanese history that will explored later in the chapter. The likelihood is high that Shigeru Mizuki (b. 1922)[293], Rumiko Takahashi and Hayao Miyazaki (b.1941) and many other authors owe many of their Yōkai and preternatural characters to Yanagita's study. There is no doubt that Yanagita's encyclopedic knowledge contributed greatly to the deep and insightful themes and dynamic and spectacular descriptions of the supernatural world that these anime and manga authors created. The spooky and unique characters in the post Second World War anime and manga stories are modeled after the preternatural beings which lived in the Yōkai world during the centuries and introduced by Yanagita[294].

Yanagita also argues in his book *Yokai Dangi* (1956)[295] that Yōkai and Kami or Shinto deities were originally the same spieces. According to his theory, these two categories were originally identical in the same way as angels and demons have the same origin in the Judeo-Christian world. Yōkai and Kami have amazing similarities through many Yōkai characters that originated in Buddhist mythology as opposed to Shinto. For instance, quite a few Yōkai and Kami characters were originally

293   Wikipedia: Shigeru Mizuki. http://en.wikipedia.org/wiki/Shigeru_Mizuki
294   Kunio Yanagita. Yōkai Dangi. (Tokyo: Kodansha, 1956)
295   Kunio Yanagita. Ibid.

human and animal spirits. They transformed into very powerful prerternatural beings either posthumously or while they were alive. It was up to various people to determine whether they are labeled as Kami or Yōkai. The demarcation between these two categories has been very ambiguous throughout the whole of Japanese history, in which many fox and raccoon dog deities are treated as both Kami and Yōkai. Likewise, in Miyazaki's *Princess Mononoke* (1997)[296], most mutated animals are treated as both Kami and Yōkai.

Nevertheless, these ghosts and spiritual beings are classified as Kami if they are beneficial to the living humans, otherwise they are referred to as Yōkai. By comparison, in Judeo-Christian narratives, demons were angels who rebelled against God and were then expelled from the heavenly realm. Unlike Judeo-Christian traditions, Japanese culture, without a monotheistic concept is extremely anthrocentric and the degree of benefit to humanity is the only creteria which determines good or bad.

In Miyazaki's movie entitled *Pom Poko*[297], the island nation without a monotheistic belief system labels deities that are harmful to humanity as Yōkai or nearly identical creatures as the fallen angels in the Judeo-Christian belief system, while worshiping gods who only appear as beneficial to them at any given time or place. Miyazaki describes an irony that raccoon dogs are still revered and worshipped as Kami in the distant island of Shikoku, while they are treated as Yōkai and pest animals in Tama district of Tokyo. From an environmentalist perspective, Miyazaki suggests that humans are the most dreadful Yōkai and monsters that are destroying the habitats of

---

296   Wikipedia: Princess Mononoke. ibid.
297   Wikipedia: Pom Poko. Online at http://en.wikipedia.org/wiki/Pom_Poko

all other species and the entire earth. At the end of this movie, many foxes and raccoon dogs with Yōkai power are blended into human society, while some without power live peacefully in the animal realm. The conclusion may suggest that some humans are coming from a Yōkai world and therefore sly, sneaky and deceptive like Nezumi Otoko in Mizuki's Kitaro series that will explore later. They have evolved and mutated into monsterous lifeforms out of the necessity to live in a harsh environment and extenuating circumstances like war.

Both Mizuki and Miyazaki carry the philosophical assumption that lives in modernity that mankind can easily ruin humanity and transform people into Yōkai. Negative and potentially destructive factors of the human world such as wars, political corruptions, discriminations and terrorism existed from antiquity. Political philosophers, religious leaders and "wisdom teachers" in both antiquity and modernity have fought vain and fruitless battles to eliminate the seed of evil that Christians see as planted in humanity in the Garden of Eden for all of history.

Despite the relentless efforts to eliminate them, evil and negative psychic energy among mankind has intensified as human civilization has advanced and the technology continues to develop. An attempt to rid evil of humanity is seems as helpless as trying to eliminate computer malfunctions manually without an antivirus program. Evil normally regenerates and multipies much more quickly than human hands can delete it. Thus, in the modern and post-modern era, these negative factors of human society increase their complications and destructiveness to both humans and other species on the planet. The modern world with an inherent ambivalence of sophistication as well as deformity will continue to dehumanize mankind and allow humans to "mutate into Yōkai."

Contemporary Yōkai Stories by Shigeru Mizuki

Shigeru Mizuki[298] is one of postwar Japan's most prolific and influential manga artist following the theme of traditional ghost stories and folklore. He described the spooky, otherworldly world of Yōkai with the time setting of late 20th and early 21st century. Mizuki is known as the author of horror manga *GeGeGe no Kitaro* (ゲゲゲの鬼太郎: 1959)[299]. He is considered a master and specialist of the genre of Yōkai tales and wrote many stories of this kind. Miziki's fascination with the Yōkai and supernatural world could have stemmed from extraordinary experiences he had as an Imperial Japanese soldier during the Second World War. In 1942, he was sent to New Britain Island in Papua New Guinea and Rabaul Island when drafted into the Imperial Japanese Army where he experienced horrors in real life. Mizuki experienced a living hell in which he wandered around the border between the domains of living and dead. While he was there as a soldier, he observed many of his friends suffer horrendous deaths. The battlefields in the southern Pacific islands seemed like gateways to Hades, and young Mizuki was forced to confront death sternly as an ultimate theme of mankind. Some had their bodies blown up and scattered into pieces while they were still alive. Unburied bodies of soldiers were eaten up by wild animals or rotted like spoiled food.

Mizuki himself contacted malaria, while watching his fellow soldiers die from battle wounds and disease. After that,

298   Wikipedia: Shigeru Mizuki. http://en.wikipedia.org/wiki/Shigeru_Mizuki
299   Wikipedia: GeGeGe no Kitaro. http://en.wikipedia.org/wiki/GeGeGe_no_Kitaro

he was also caught in an explosion during an Allied air raid and lost his left arm. He returned home from Rabaul after having a serious injury, captured and released as a prisoner of war. Also, his older brother, an artillery officer of the Imperial army, was convicted as a war criminal for having prisoners of war executed. As a left-handed person, losing his left arm was extremely difficult. After the war, he worked hard to train himself to use his right hand to draw manga. Following his return he worked as a movie theater operator until his started his career as a manga writer in 1956.

There is no doubt that Mizuki's anti-war theme in his work stemmed from his own near death experiences during the Second World War. Matthew Penney (2009) maintains that Mizuki had been critical to both Japanese and American military operations during the war. In the 1960s, he railed against the American military's practice of bombing civilian targets instead of military bases in the supernatural series Akuma-kun (悪魔くん) or *Lil' Devil*. In the late 1980s, Mizuki completed a masterpiece with picturesque graphic images said to have synthesized his own personal experiences as an imperial soldier with the grand narrative of Japan's modern history, the incident of the Nanking Massacre, descriptions of forced labor, and other Japanese war crimes. It became a bestseller and was awarded with the Kodansha Manga Prize, one of the industry's highest accolades[300]. After viewing Mizuki's manga and anime movies, one might easily come to the conclusion that all wars and military operations conceive the demonic nature within. As humans often evolve or devolve

---

300   Matthew Penney. War and Japan: The Non-Fiction Manga of Mizuki Shigeru: The Asian Pacific Journal: Japan Focus, 2009. Online at http://japanfocus.org/-Matthew_Penney/2905

into Yōkai in some folklore, war easily transforms humanity into a horrendous monster. Mizuki's war narratives send a message that every human individual have opportunities to mutate into Yōkai, a creature that is often used to represent the dark side of humanity.

GeGeGe no Kitaro, Mizuki's most wellknown masterpiece is a manga and TV anime series created in 1959. It describes the depth of Yōkai world in Japanese folklore, although the time setting is contemporary Japan. Kitaro the protagonist is a Yōkai boy born in a cemetery whose left eye is missing, but his hair usually covers the empty socket. He fights for peace between humans and Yōkai using his supernatural power similar to InuYasha except Kitaro does not use it that much since the time setting is contemporary. His combat usually involves protecting vulnerable humans from the overwhelmingly powerful Yōkai force. In the original manga story in 1959, Kitaro was born in the modern world. However, in the 2007 real time movie he was an over 300 years old man born in the Edo Period who looked like a young boy. When questioned in the movie, Kitaro responds that he is 350 years old, that is about 100 years junior to InuYasha. Readers could understand Kitaro as the alter ego of young Mizuki, who lived in the Yōkai world or the battle field, though it does not include wartime stories.

Other fascinating Yōkai character of this series include Kitaro's father, *Nezumi Otoko* (ねずみ男) or "Rat Man", *Neko Musume* (猫娘) or "Cat Girl". Kitaro's father is called *Medama-oyaji* (目玉のおやじ) or "Eyeball Father". He was once a fully-formed Yōkai who looked like an adult human, but his entire body perished of a disease except for an eyeball. After that, he was reborn out of his decayed body as an anthropomorphic version of his own eyeball. Medama-oyaji also lost his wife who was Kitaro's mother, when the disease annihilated the whole village. He looks small and fragile, but has a strong will and cares for his son greatly. In some English translations he is referred to as *Daddy Eyeball*. He might have a different name when he had a fully-formed body, but the story did not mention it. He often assists Kitaro to fight a battle against evil monsters with his encyclopedic knowledge about the Yōkai world[301].

Nezumi Otoko is a greedy, unprincipled and opportunist Yōkai character who plays an important part in the Kitaro series. He is a hanyō or yōkai-human halfbreed similar to InuYasha and posesses rodent-like facial features and a humanoid body. While Nezumi Otoko is usually a friend of Kitaro and his company, he is often treacherous, betraying them if he thinks it is more profitable to take the side of evildoers or powerful enemies of Kitaro. He is 350 years old in both manga and anime series, and lives a peculiar lifestyle almost never taking a bath, rendering him filthy, foul-smelling, and covered in welts and sores. He claims to hold a degree from a college for Yōkai called *Kaiki Daigaku* (怪奇大学) having studied the supernatural matters and Yōkai history[302]. However, his knowledge about the Yōkai world is not comparable to Kitaro's father who possesses an extraordinary knowledge and insights.

Nezumi Otoko could be modeled after greedy and crooked merchants called *yamiya* (闇屋) who were prevalent in Japan shortly after the Second World War. The literal meaning of the term *yamiya* means "those who practice business in

301   Wikipedia: GeGeGe no Kitaro. Ibid.
302   Wikipedia: GeGeGe no Kitaro. Ibid.

darkness", since yami (闇) refers to the absence of light. Japan was extremely poor in those days and nearly all life sustaining products were in short supply. Consumers were required to present a ticket issued from the government along with cash when they purchased food. These merchants usually obtained products illegally and sold them to customers without food tickets for outrageously high prices. Consumers had no choice other than purchasing food from *yamiya,* spending a fortune, since the government issued a very limited number of the tickets.

This was a period when the morality sharply declined in the nation, since people in the whole archipelago became apathetic after their defeat in the Second World War. Mizuki closely observed Japanese society including the greedy and unethical business practitioners like Nezumi Otoko. To him, they were filthy, unclean creatures like rodents, who possessed no moral discernment, yet still retained humanity. These merchants were people like the Yōkai who abandoned human conscience after experiencing extreme pain, stress or grief during the war. In a sense, they have transformed into the Yōkai like *Naraku* in the InuYasha series after the nation was defeated in the war. Nezumi Otoko has some similarities to Naraku although the former is not as evil as the latter. They both are classified as *hanyō* or half-human and half- yōkai, though Naraku has a past that he was fully human. They both have a human conscience within, but they have evil deeds since the overwhelmingly powerful Yōkai nature is suppressing their humanity.

Another significant character is *Neko Musume* (猫娘) or "Cat Girl", who modeled after a bakeneko (化け猫), a typical feline Yōkai in Japanese folklore. She normally takes the form of an ordinary young human female except her eyes resemble cat eyes, and she is capable of turning into a powerful Yōkai when she is in a battle or hunting mode. Normally a quiet Yōkai girl, she transforms into a frightening feline monster with fangs and shiny cat-like eyes when she is angry or hungry for prey[303]. Because of her feline nature, she does not get along well with Nezumi Otoko, who is a rodent. She seems to have a romantic interest in Kitaro, who sees her only as a friend. As mentioned in the previous chapter, Japanese folklore includes various feline Yōkai because of the charming, mysterious and occasionally frightening nature of the spieces. Like *Kirara* in InuYasha series, Neko Musume often reveals the furious Yōkai nature and assists Kitaro when he is in trouble, though normally she maintains a humanoid mode with feline features. She is hanyō or half-human and half-yōkai like Nezumi Otoko, so that she also possesses human emotions and mindset, unlike Kirara.

Less significant minor characters in the Kitaro series include *Sunakake Babaa* (砂かけ婆) or "Sand-throwing Old Woman", *Konaki Jijii* (子泣き爺) or "Child-crying Old Man", *Ittan Momen* (一反木綿) or "Roll of Cotton", and Nurikabe (ぬりかべ) or "Plastered Wall". These minor characters in the Kitaro series are taken from traditional folklore from many different regions of the country. They are good Yōkai characters and Kitaro's close friends, which assist him to fight the battle against evil and have occasional appearances in the story as semi-regular characters[304].

---

303   Wikipedia: GeGeGe no Kitaro. Ibid.
304   Wikipedia: GeGeGe no Kitaro. Ibid.

Sunakake Babaa is a female Yōkai with the appearance of an old woman who carries sand which she throws into the eyes of enemies to blind them. She serves as an advisor to Kitaro and his company when they fight a battle, and manages an apartment building for Yōkai. The character stems from an invisible sand-throwing spirit from the folklore of Nara and Hyogo prefectures[305]. She often sprinkles sand over people and theretens them when they are walking around Shinto shrines and other solitary places. According to some legends, the true identity of Sunakake Babaa is a Tanuki or racoon dog. Tanuki and other carnivorous spieces have a habit of throwing sand using their rear feet. This interpretation is also completely understandable because Tanuki possesses supernatural power to do several amazing things including transformation into humans and many other objects in Japanese legends. In Japanese history, Tanuki and other canines like foxes, wolves and domestic dogs are treated as Yōkai and even gods with supernatural forces for more than a millennium. Therefore, it is easy to conclude that Sunakake Babaa could be considered an anthropomorphic form of Tanuki Yōkai. No matter how this character originated, Mizuki transformed her into a Yōkai of Justice fighting against the evil Yōkai and the power of darkness[306].

Konaki Jijii (子泣き爺) or "Child-crying Old Man" is a comical, absent-minded Yōkai with an appearance of an old man who attacks enemies by clinging to them and turning himself to stone, increasing his weight immensely and pinning them down. He and Sunakake Babaa often team up and fight

---

305   Wikipedia: GeGeGe no Kitaro. Ibid.
306   Wikipedia: 砂かけ婆. Online at http://ja.wikipedia.org/wiki/%E7%A0%82%E3%81%8B%E3%81%91%E5%A9%86

together. The character of Konaki Jijii is modelled after a ghost who appears in the woods of Tokushima Prefecture in the form of a crying baby. According to the legend, when some traveler picks up the baby, the weight increases until crushing the person to death. In an old story in Tokushima Prefecture, probably prior to the Edo Period, Konaki Jijii was a person who existed in the real history. He was a strange elderly man who likely suffered a mental illness and imitated the voice of an infant while wandering around the village. Because of his odd and somewhat psychotic behaviour, the neighbours in the same community feared him, keeping their children from him, and named him Konaki Jijii or "Child-crying Old Man". Today, when children are disobedent, their parents often threaten them by telling, "You are sent to Konaki Jijii"[307]. In some other districts of the same prefecture, there was also a legend of a female version called *Konaki Babaa* (子泣き婆) or "Child-crying Old Woman" with almost identical attributes and features as Konaki Jijii. Some others argue that the legend of Konaki Jijii existed in neither antiquity nor medieval ages, but was created in the modern era after the the Meiji Restoration. Although the origin of Konaki Jijii as a Yōkai character is obscure, many modern authors after the Second World War wrote stories about him. In the same way as Sunakake Babaa, Mizuki transformed him into a Yōkai of Justice though originally a trouble maker for humanity in the Kitaro series[308].

Ittan Momen (一反木綿) or "Roll of Cotton" is a flying Yōkai resembling a strip of white cotton cloth. Kitaro and his colleagues often ride on him when traveling. This character is

---

307   Wikipedia: GeGeGe no Kitaro. Ibid.
308   Wikipedia: 子泣き爺. Online at http://ja.wikipedia.org/wiki/%E5%AD%90%E6%
B3%A3%E3%81%8D%E7%88%BA

modeled after a mythological flying monster from Kagoshima Prefecture that wraps itself around the faces of humans in an attempt to smother them. *Nurikabe* (ぬりかべ) or "Plastered Wall" is a large wall-shaped Yōkai from Fukuoka Prefecture, who uses his massive size to protect Kitaro and his company. These two are rather flat characters without distinct personalities treated by the author as less significant characters than Sunakake Babaa and Konaki Jijii, though friends and comrades of Kitaro[309].

In 2011, Mizuki published an illustrated reference book entitled "Shigeru Mizuki's Yōkai Map" which introduced various Yōkai characters from different regions of Japan[310]. The book deals with a wide scope of the Yōkai world from antiquity to modern days that includes *Sunakake Babaa*, *Konaki Jijii* and *Ittan Momen* that he introduced in *GeGeGe no Kitaro* series. There is no doubt that his study was inspired by Yanagita who investigated the preternatural world extensively in the previous century.

Raccoon Dog War in Miyazaki's Pom Poko

It is also significant that Hayao Miyazaki[311] illustrated Tanuki or raccoon dogs as Yōkai that exercise supernatural power in the modern world. In *Heisei Tanuki Gassen Pom Poko* (平成狸合戦ぽんぽこ), his animated film released in 1994, Miyazaki portrayed Tanuki as a highly sociable, mischievous species, able to use "illusion science" to transform into almost anything including humans and other animals. The time setting of the movie was 1970s Japan in which a group of tanuki is

---

309   Wikipedia: GeGeGe no Kitaro. Ibid.
310   Shigeru Mizuki. Mizuki Shigeru no Yokai Chizu. (Shigeru Mizuki's Yōkai Map) (Tokyo: Hebonsha, 2011)
311   Wikipedia: Hayao Miyazaki. ibid.

threatened by a gigantic and ongoing suburban development project called *New Tama* on the western side of Tokyo. The development is brutally cutting into their forest habitat every year, and destroying the living space and food of these raccoon dogs and other wild animals[312].

Finally, a group of raccoon dogs supported by elders from various regions from the country declare the war against humanity using supernatural force, since humans are polluting the environment and destroying their habitat. Several prominent tanuki characters lead the resistance force, including the militant Gonta, the old guru Tsurugame, the wise-woman Oroku, and the young Shoukichi who is the protagonist and narrator. They are highly organized and employ various strategies and tactics to stop people from destroying the forest by creating illusions and causing fears. These attacks are initially quite effective, injure and even kill some people and frightening many construction workers into quitting their jobs. However, more workers soon replace them. For those employing the use of supernatural force, it exhausts their energy quickly, since it requires large amount of psychic power. When Tanuki remains in humans or any form other than the original raccoon dogs, they have to keep on drinking energy drink made of Akamamushi (赤まむし) or "Red Viper"[313].

After the arrival of all elders from remote regions, the entire group in Tama district plans a massive "ghost parade" to make the human residents think the growing town is haunted and to re-establish respect for the supernatural among them.

---

312   Wikipedia: Pom Poko. Online at http://en.wikipedia.org/wiki/Pom_Poko
313   Japanese energy drinks generally contain extracts from various exotic species like snakes, soft-shell turtles, Ginseng and other herbal plants, while North Americal counterparts are a simply massive amount of caffeine.

The strain of the massive illusion requires a tremendous amount of psychic power and kills one of the elders as a result. The effort also seems failed when the owner of a nearby theme park falsely takes credit for the parade, claiming the entire incident was only a publicity stunt. After that, their strength is exhausted and their efforts to stop the development project fails. They also discover that foxes, another species with the power to transform according to Japanese folklore, has already been blended into human society and are living as mankind. Some Tanuki leaders suggest they should follow the example of the foxes, join the human world and live like them. However, many members of the group are reluctant to choose this alternative because they would then have to abandon the comrades without power to transform.

Toward the end of the story, the most aggressive fraction among Tanuki residents led by Gonta fight a fierce battle against humans and die like traditional Samurai warriors. They impersonate the appearance of a group of militant enviormentalists protesting against the development and interfere with the construction. However, when the police force becomes involved, they are brutally slaughtered for the act of civil disobedience. When they die, they return to the original form of raccoon dogs and are simply disposed of as the remains of pest animals. After the battle is over, the tanuki who are most fully trained to transform and create illusion are left with no choice but to live as humans in the city just as foxes do, abandoning those who have no power to transform. Those without power continue to live as animals in the forest that is now significantly smaller than before completion of the New Tama development project. At the end of the movie, Shoukichi, who now lives as a human, is returning home by commuter train after a long day. Tired from work, walking home with his Akamamushi energy drink in his hand, he discovers a familiar Tanuki group having a party in an open field on his neighbour's property. He returns to the Tanuki form, throwing off his suit and joining the party, since they were his childhood friends with whom he grew up[314].

Naruto the Contemporary Ninja Story
& Preternatural World

Naruto (1997)[315] is another product of Japanese modern day's pop-culture that demonstrates the motif of the preternatural world and occultic and psychic power. It is an ongoing Japanese manga and anime series with modern day's Ninja (忍者) theme written by Masashi Kishimoto (b. 1974)[316]. In this manga and anime series, Ninja characters who live in a community named *Hidden Leaf Village* or *Konohagakure no Sato* (木ノ葉隠れの里), perform spectacular Ninjutsu (忍術) or Ninja arts that manipulate natural and supernatural elements with psychic power and destroy powerful enemies in the contemporary time setting. Many other Ninja stories are based on the feudal Sengoku Period in the 15th century or the same historical setting as InuYasha. These Ninja characters with superhuman power perform various mysterious and occultic arts and defeat enemies by manipulating elements like water, fire and wind. Some of abilities of these characters include invisibility, walking on water, and control over natural elements.

314   Wikipedia: ibid.
315   Wikipedia: Naruto. Online at http://en.wikipedia.org/wiki/Naruto
316   Wikipedia: Masashi Kishimoto. Online at http://en.wikipedia.org/wiki/Masashi_Kishimoto

However, a Ninja, or Shinobi, originally referred to a covert agent or mercenary of the Sengoku era after the late Muromachi Period who specialized in unconventional arts of war. Nevertheless, people who lived during the relatively peaceful and prosperous Edo Period romanticized these enigmatic warriors from the past and transformed them into heroes with superhuman attributes. By the time of the Meiji Restoration (1868), the tradition of the Shinobi had become a topic of popular culture and imaginative stories. Today's Ninja stories are mostly based on folklore and legend, and therefore, it is often difficult to separate historical fact from myth. As a consequence, the perception of the Ninja world in the popular culture of the West is based more on the legend and folklore than on any historical spies of the Sengoku Period[317].

The protagonist of Kishimoto's story is Naruto Uzumaki (渦巻ナルト), an adolescent Ninja who constantly pursues recognition from his peer and aspires to become a powerful Ninja like his late father Minato Namikaze (波風ミナト) the Fourth Hokage. Minato is the most powerful Ninja in Hidden Leaf Village and acknowledged as the leader of the community and the strongest of all. Naruto dreams that someday he might become a great Ninja like Minato and inherit the very honoured title Hokage from his father. Naruto is an inspirational character among youths and young adults worldwide probably because of his optimism, positive thinking and ceaceless pursuit of his dream. He was originally a mischevous, undisciplined, troubled teen who grew up in the village without parents[318].

---

317   Wikipedia: Ninja. Online at http://en.wikipedia.org/wiki/Ninja
318   Narutopedia, the Naruto Encyclopedia Wiki: Naruto Uzumaki. Online at http://en.wikipedia.org/wiki/Naruto

The Naruto series contains various themes coming from traditional Japanese spirituality and pre-modern mysticism such as reincarnation and the power of Chakra which enables Ninja characters to manipulate natural and supernatural elements of the universe. Some Ninja and Non-Ninja characters struggle with karma from the previous existences, but Naruto constantly urges to overcome it with positive thinking and efforts to discard baggage from the past. It seems that Kishimoto has incorporated the concept of "positive thinking" coming from the contemporary school of pop psychology. Naruto acts as a psycho-therapist to overcome karma from the past and other life controlling problems, just as the *Waki* in Zeami Motokiyo's *Noh* theatre played a very significant role to pacify the angry spirits in the Muromachi Period.

As an infant, Nine-Tailed Fox Yōkai (九尾の妖狐) is sealed inside of Naruto's body, when Minato, his father and the village leader defeated, at the expense of his life, the evil Yōkai who terrorized the entire village. The Third Hokage, the master of Naruto's father who replaced the leadership of his late student made a decree to ban anyone to mention the attack of Nine-Tailed Fox Yōkai to anyone else. He did so to protect the son of his best student from those who regarded Naruto as if he were the fox monster itself. Because of this, Naruto himself is not aware of the Yōkai inside of him[319]. Naruto's mother also died when he was very young, so that he grew up as an orphan. While he attends Ninja Academy, he becomes stronger and more competent in Ninja skills and grows as a person[320].

319   Narutopedia, the Naruto Encyclopedia Wiki: Naruto Uzumaki. Ibid.
320   Shonen Jump's Naruto Anime Profiles Episodes 1-37. (Tokyo: Shonen Jump, 2010)

It is believed Inari Ōkami can become the enemy of humanity like the Nine-Tailed Fox in the Naruto series if people mismanage it, though it is usually friendly and beneficial to people.

Naruto joins an elete Genin (下忍) or Junior Ninja Squad led by Master Kakashi Hatake (はたけカカシ) later after he completes the academy and the elders of the village recognize his competency, unusually strong character, and very powerful *chakra* probably coming from the Fox Yōkai within. His team-mates in the squad are Sakura Haruno and Sasuke Uchiha (うちはサスケ) who are members of the Uchiha clan. Sasuke was Naruto's rival and the two youths do not get along well when they originally join the squad named Team 7. Sasuke, an orphan like Naruto, is one of the last members from the Uchiha clan from the village of Konohagakure. When Naruto first encounters Sasuke in the Ninja Academy of the village, they are matched to spar against each other. However, Sasuke and Naruto become more sympathetic to each other as the story progresses. When Naruto finds out Sasuke was an orphan like him, he is secretly happy that he is not the only one alone and wants to talk to him[321].

According to folklore, Sasuke's character was likely modeled after Sarutobi Sasuke (猿飛佐助), a legendary Ninja who lived during the late Muromachi period. Both Naruto and Sasuke came from prestigious Ninja lineages; however grew up as orphans since both their parents suffered tragic deaths. In the Ninja Academy, Sasuke was a straight A student, while Naruto's grade was the lowest. Several other young Ninja

---

321   Narutopedia, the Naruto Encyclopedia Wiki: Naruto Uzumaki. Ibid.

recruits in the *Hidden Leaf Village* include Shikamura Nara, Ino Yamanaka, Choji Akimichi, Hinata Hyuga and Kiba Inuzaka.

Master Kakashi a very powerful Ninja with the highest rank, who initially appears aloof and enigmatic, takes up the role to train these three youngsters and teaches them Ninja skills and patiently mentors them. Kakashi recognizes the potential that Naruto would become a very powerful Ninja like his father and his master Third Kokage even though he barely graduates and his grades are very low.

Concept of Chakra in Naruto Series

Chakra is the major theme that is constantly referred to throughout the Naruto series and other Ninja stories. In the Naruto world, Ninja characters in addition to Nijutsu (忍術) perform various Jutsu or skills like Genjutsu (幻術), Doujutsu (瞳術) and Taijutsu (体術) that historical Ninja exercise. In the Ninja Academy, students are taught the art of controling Chakra to defeat the enemy as the most important subject matter, although the training of the historical Ninja figures was mostly physical and martial art disciplines such as long distance runs, climbing, stealth methods of walking and swimming. It is a supernatural force practised by Ninja, Yōkai and various other preternatural characters in a wide range of Asian mythologies, folklore from the antiquity and modern science fictions. In general, Chakra is the hybrid energy produced, when physical and spiritual energies are mixed together. In In this Ninja World, when a Ninja uses Chakra, he or she must wear Hand Seals to protect him or herself from the potential damage of overusing the power of Chakra. Master Kakashi recognized that Naruto had a potential to make a higher achievement than Sakura and Sasuke as a Ninja though his grade at school was unspeakably low, because he sensed much more powerful Chakra coming from the young boy than a couple of his team-mates or any other recent graduates of the academy[322].

Hand Seals are used by Ninja to activate Chakra and perform most attacks. Simple and entry level Jutsu are are based on the configurations of 12 animals of the Chinese Zodiac (十二支) like the Rat, Ox, Tiger, Rabbit, Dragon, Snake, Horse, Sheep, Monkey, Rooster, Dog and Pig. However, many of the more complicated and advanced combat skills have unique finishing Hand Seals not based on Zodiac animals. Most Chakra practitioners combine two Hand Seals with the use of both hands. Nevertheless, some advanced Chakra users like Haku are able to perform Hand Seals with only one hand. However, it was a very rare example, and even Kakashi had never seen anything like this before[323].

Chakra has several different types in the Naruto series. Normal Chakra is the ordinary, average type of Chakra that everyone is born with and Ninja are trained very early on to learn to control it. The second type is *Celestial Gates Chakra*, in which a Ninjutsu practitioner can access one hundred percent of their total power by breaking all of the body's limits on how much strength can be used. The restrictions of this type of Chakra are known as Gates, eight gates in all. Since this kind of Chakra combined with physical muscles is so powerful, using them to their full capacity will destroy the practitioner's body, literally making the muscles explode or rip into pieces. Therefore, this Chakra can only be used briefly or no longer

---

322   Naruto2: Naruto Chakra Guide. Online at http://www.naruto2.com/Information/
Chakra_Guide/Naruto-ChakraGuide_Main.aspx
323   Naruto2: Naruto Chakra Guide. Ibid.

than five minutes. Otherwise, it kills the user since all gates
which allow the energy force to flow have been unlocked.
The fewer gates that are unlocked, the longer the Ninja can
continue to use Chakra until the attack kills them. Because the
Celestial Gates Chakra attack is so powerful and dangerous,
it is classified as a forbidden jutsu. Another dangerous Chakra
that is normally forbidden is the *Cursed Seal Chakra*. This
kind of Chakra may only be used if the user has been given
the *Cursed Seal* and survived the ten percent chance of
being killed from it, and can only be accessed after all of the
person's normal chakra has been drained[324].

According to the *Naruto2* web site, Chakra in the Naruto
world is somewhat similar to energy forms demonstrated in
Dragonball[325], another well known anime and manga series
created by Akira Toriyama (b. 1955)[326] as well as several other
popular anime stories. Naruto and other Ninja recruits go
through intense and harsh training and spend an excessively
long time to accomplish their goals both in the academy and
following graduation. The article in the web site also maintains
that the slow process of the Chakra acquisition in the Naruto
world prevents misuse by a 12 year old with enough energy to
blow up a whole planet[327].

In Dragonball anime and manga series, the protagonist
is a young monkey-tailed boy named Goku who belongs to
a powerful alien species named Saiyans. Throughout the
series, he grows into adulthood, gets married to a human
female and procreates children and grandchildren as the

---

324   Naruto2: Naruto Chakra Guide. Ibid.
325   Wikipedia: Dragon Ball. Online at http://en.wikipedia.org/wiki/Dragon_ball
326   Wikipedia: Akira Toriyama. Online at http://en.wikipedia.org/wiki/Akira_Toriyama
327   Naruto2: Naruto Chakra Guide. Ibid.

series progresses. Goku goes through an unending cycle of fighting, winning, losing and improving himself in the same way as Naruto. As he grows older and continues to train himself, he increases in power and strength so that he is able to kill mightier enemies. Nevertheless, as a Saiyan, he already possesses an enoumous power that no humans ever had when he was born[328].

However, Naruto and his team-mates take a longer time and more intense training to build up Chakra than Goku or any other Saiyan characters in Dragonball, since they were mere humans. Naruto is a little closer to Goku than Sakura and Sasuke, since he inherited the strength from the Nine-Tailed Fox Yōkai. However, his power is incomparable with Goku who is a Saiyan. At the same time, the Naruto theme of Chakra parallels with the intense physical training and extraordinary mental discipline of the historical Ninja warrior who was a covert agent of feudal Japan. In the Naruto world, young Ninja trainees learn better ways to use their Chakra through intense physical training as well, under the strict supervision of Kakashi.

In particular, Kakashi demands his students to practice tree climbing to increase Chakra and physical strength. In this exercise, the trainee must concentrate Chakra at the bottom of the feet, and walk up a tree as if it were ground. If he or she has too much Chakra in the feet, he will break the tree and fall to the ground. If he or she has too little Chakra, the person will also fall. If the practitioner has the appropriate amount he or she will stick to the tree. According to Kakashi's theory, if his students can sustain the right amount long enough to walk to

---

328   Wikipedia: Dragon Ball. Ibid.

the top of a tree, they have learned the exercise and the goal is accomplished[329].

The contrast between the two anime characters can be said to be comparable to the difference between the Apollo, the deity and Achilles the human hero in Greek mythology. Apollo[330] is fully divine and equipped with superhuman attributes in the same way as Goku the Saiyan. They both are immortal and invincible, being completely distinct from the mortals. For both Goku and Apollo, superhuman endowments are like birthrights since they are essentially different from humans. Both of them also have half-human children who are more powerful than ordinary humans, but not comparable to their fully divine fathers. Since they are essentially mortals, they age more quickly and are destined to die much earlier than their fathers.

On the other hand, Achilles[331] is the son of the nymph Thetis and Peleus, the king of the Myrmidons. He is made as invincible as Apollo except his feet became known as having "Achilles tendon." Achilles had almost divine or superhuman qualities, but is essentially mortal and incomparable to fully divine characters in physical and mental strength. In the same way, Naruto who possesses a fox monster within has a little higher Chakra and athletic abilities than any peers in Ninja Academy, but is not invincible and requires ceaceless training and strong discipline to achieve his goals. Both Achilles and Naruto are comparable with the half-human offsprings of Apollo and Goku since they simultaneously possess super-human attributes and the fragility of humanity.

329   Naruto2: Naruto Chakra Guide. Ibid.
330   Wikipedia: Apollo. Online at http://en.wikipedia.org/wiki/Dragon_ball
331   Wikipedia: Achilles. Online at http://en.wikipedia.org/wiki/Achilles

According to Robert J. Rabel[332] (1990), Apollo is a Model
for Achilles in Homer's[333] Iliad[334], since the two characters are
often portrayed in strikingly similar fashion. In other words,
Achilles is a knock off or degraded version of Apollo who is
perfect and spotless. Throughout the Iliad's scenes of battle,
these two are implacable enemies. As a defender of Troy,
Apollo strikes Patroclus, who is wearing Achilles' armour, and
becomes the cause of his death. Later, Apollo diverts Achilles
from his slaughter of the Trojans, allowing many to escape
within the city's walls, and tricks the mortal hero who responds
with a wish for revenge. Later, as Hector, the Trojan prince,
prophesies of his death, Achilles is slain by Paris and Apollo
outside the gates of Troy.

According to Rabel, one of the largest themes of Iliad
is the contrast of mortality and immortality. Apollo and
Achilles both exercise the power of divine anger targeted at
Agamemnon, the commander-in-chief of the Greeks during the
Trojan War, although they are uncompromising enemies. Rabel
also contends that Apollo blames Achilles for the ruthlessness
and lack of compassion during the battle and provides the
appropriate warning to remember his mortality. Achilles humbly
accepts the warning from the deity of whom he was modelled.
Rabel draws the conclusion that the hero not only discovers
but even learns to take enjoyment in the limitations of his
mortality by confronting Apollo, learning it is futile attempt to
transcend in imitation of a god. He contends that the hero

332   Robert J. Rabel. Apollo as a Model for Achilles in the Iliad. The American Journal
of Philology, Volume 111, 1990. 429-440
333   Wikipedia: Homer. Online at http://en.wikipedia.org/wiki/Homer
334   Homer. Iliad (Indianapolis/Cambridge: Hackett Publishing Company, 1977)

most closely resembles the divinity when he fully embraces his own humanity in the final paradox of the Iliad[335].

Likewise, Naruto's personality develops significantly as he repeats failures and increases the awareness of the fragile nature of his human self throughout the series. Naruto establishes a stronger ego identity and adult self as well as a professional identity as a Shinobi when he goes through trials and tribulations. In other words, he develops his new identity as a person in an Eriksonian sense as he strives to increase his Chakra and professional competency. Erik Erikson (1902 – 1994)[336] maintained that with the establishment of a good relationship to the world of skills and to those who teach and share the new skills, childhood comes to an end, so Naruto rapidly moves to the new stage of his life while he is in an apprenticeship under Kakashi[337].

Unlike Achilles, Naruto has a humbling experience in his early life since he does not start his career as elite of the society and takes a much longer time to be recognized than the Greek hero. Although he had stronger Chakra than his teammates and other Ninja recruits in the Hidden Leaf Village, his grade in the academy is the lowest. However, his character is inspirational partly due to his weakness and fragile human self. Naruto also has an extraordinary drive to overcome his weaknesses and excel in the Ninja art and aspires to be as good as his late father and obtain the title Hokage, since he has a human self. Since both Naruto and Achilles are mortals and destined to die, they both have Eriksonian seasons of life

---

335   Rabel. Ibid.
336   Wikipedia: Erik Erikson. Online at http://en.wikipedia.org/wiki/Erik_Erikson
337   Erik H. Erikson. Identity and the Life Cycle. (London, UK: W. W. Norton & Company, Inc, 1959/1980)

and themes of adolescent development and distinct factors which make them more attractive than deities and immortals.

[338]Naruto Uzumaki & Sasuke Uchiha[339].

---

338   Was available November 2011: http://akg.cscblog.jp/content/0000389127.html
339   The picture is used under "fair dealing" (Canada) and "fair use" (USA) provisions in copyright law.

5

Christianity in Modern Japan

Japanese Christianity that was begun by Roman Catholics enjoyed freedom briefly after the Meiji Restoration (明治維新) which began in 1868. In the Meiji Period, Protestant denominations entered the archipelago for the first time and started their work vigorously. Missionary activities from both Catholic and Protestant organizations flourished after the ban enforced by Tokugawa shogunate was lifted. Ironically, the majority of new converts were former shogunate officials who belonged to Samurai class and lost jobs after the restoration. Once converted to the Christianity, they became very dedicated, serious and passionate believers. They served Christ as their new master in the same way as they previously served Shogun following the Samurai ethics. Some of them were so ambitious that they went overseas and pursued foreign education and started Christian schools.

Christianity & State Shinto

However, Christians in Japan soon learned that the Meiji government was not any more open to them than Tokugawa shogunate. New persecution was about to come after the promulgation of the *Meiji Constitution*[340] and enactment of

---

340   Wikipedia: Meiji Constitution. Online at http://en.wikipedia.org/wiki/Meiji_Constitution

the [341]*Imperial Rescript on Education* in the name of the emperor. The constitution came into existence on 11 February 1889 and the Rescript in the following year. From Article 1-3, the Meiji Constitution was founded on the principle that sovereignty resided in the person of the Emperor by virtue of his divine ancestry "unbroken for ages eternal," rather than in the people." The Rescript was made for the public educational system and emphasized the Confucian virtues of loyalty and filial piety as well as the sacredness of the emperor[342].

Christians were forced to agree with the constitution and the educational rescript that stipulated the divinity of the emperor and contradicted with Christian principles. Some yielded to the pressure and compromised their beliefs and accepted the sacredness of the emperor, though others openly expressed their disagreement and faced persecution.

In the Shōwa Period (昭和時代: 1926 - 1989), during the reign of Emperor Hirohito (1901 – 1989), the freedom of religion was becoming even more restricted because the State Shinto and the military increased in power. [343]Furthermore, the government of Japan under Prime Minister [344]Kiichiro Hiranuma who was also one of 14 convicted Class-A War criminals, enacted the notorious *Religious Organization Law* in 1940. Under this law, the government was able to control all religious matter of every regulating religious organization as it did all corporations. Religious organizations had to apply for and be granted government recognition to operate legally. The

---

341   Wikipedia: Imperial Prescript on Education. Online at http://en.wikipedia.org/wiki/Imperial_Rescript_on_Education
342   Ebihara. Shinto War Gods of Yasukuni Shrine. ibid.
343   O'Brien and Ohsaki. To dream of dreams : religious freedom and constitutional politics in postwar Japan, p. 46
344   Kiichiro Hiranuma was one of 14 convicted Class-A War criminal. He died in prison in 1952, was enshrined as *Kami* in Yasukuni Shrine.

recognition depended on the religious body's agreement with the teaching and rites and support of the emperor's divinity. Many pastors did comply with the government's demand and participated in the rituals of the Shinto Shrine. They defended their actions as participation in the "Shinto style non religious rituals." Some of them went so far as to incorporate the Imperial Rescript on Education into their sermons[345].

Under the *Religious Organization Law* set by the government of Kiichiro Hiranuma, Christianity and many other minority religions were ruthlessly persecuted. All religious organizations had to apply for and be granted government recognition to operate legally. The recognition depended on the religious body's agreement to teach rites supportive of the emperor's divinity. Unfortunately, many pastors complied with the government's demand and participated in the rituals of Shinto Shrine. These organizations were forced to accommodate their philosophies of religion in order to support or at least not contradict the philosophy of the emperor as divine and descended from the sun-goddess and other Shinto based worldviews[346].

Forced Syncretism between Christianity & Shinto

Because of the Meiji Constitution and Imperial Rescript on Education during the 19th Century and the infamous Religious Organization Law enacted shortly before the Second World War, some Japanese Christians were pressured to a serious doctrinal compromise. As the result, a syncretism between Christianity and Shinto belief system and Japan's nationalism

---

345   Ebihara. Shinto War Gods of Yasukuni Shrine. ibid.
346   Hiranuma's deeds were even more evil than 7 of them who were sentenced to death and hanged in 1948. (In my personal opinion, Prime Minister Tojo who was hanged in 1948 was much better person than Hiranuma). Yet surprisingly, he was sentenced to life imprisonment instead.

also existed. [347] D.C. Holtom contends that in the early summer of 1939, [348]Akira Ebisawa, who was at the time the executive secretary of the *National Christian Council of Japan,* made a stunning statement that the Japanese Empire was the earthly manifestation of the Kingdom of God. Central to his argument was the identification of the Christian conception of the Kingdom of God on earth with the extension of Japanese political sway in eastern Asia. Ebisawa wrote that:

> What is then the place for the long-term reconstruction of East Asia? Its purpose is that of realizing the vision emblazoned on the banner, "The world one family"; and that purpose, we must recognize afresh, coincides spontaneously with the fundamental faith of Christianity. The policy of extending even to the continent our family principle which finds its centre in an Imperial House so that all may bathe in its holy benevolence — this policy, can we not see? — is none other than the concrete realization on earth of spiritual family principle of Christianity which looks up to God as the Father of mankind and regards all men as brethren. This is the Christian conception of the Kingdom of God (Ebisawa, 1939).

For Ebisawa, it was a duty and opportunity to support the great extension of the empire and promote "Japanism" to be true to the inner spiritual nature and devoted to high moral purposes.

Holtom noted that according to *Kojiki,* the very beginning of the account of the creation of the world included a deity called *Ame-no-Minakanushi-no-Kami* which meant "Lord of

---

347   D.C. Holtom. Modern Japan and Shinto Nationalism. (New York: USA Paragon Book Reprint Corp, 1963) p. 109
348   Akira Ebisawa. Tao Shinchitsujo no Kensetsu to Kirisuto Kyo, ("Christianity and Enlightenment of the New Orient in East Asia") , Bulletin of the National Christian Council of Japan, No. 183. June, 1939, p.1 (translated by Bishop A.C. Mann).

the Creator of Heaven" or [349]*Kotoamatsukami* (別天神) which meant "distinguishing heavenly kami." He was the progenitor of the entire universe, that is, all Kami including the sun goddess Amaterasu and all creatures including humans.

The syncretism of Christianity and Shinto and Japan's nationalism also helped the nation's establishment during the era of imperialism and expansionism. During this era, Japan used the *Kokutai* ideology of monotheistic universalism to bolster their actions. This included that the universal Creator God supported their actions as they were ready to invade China and other parts of East Asia. They had to "monotheize" Shinto religion to create a rationale to start the *Jihad* or Holy War in the same way Islamic terrorists claim their actions are supported by *Allah,* the Creator God. The Shinto authority tried to rationalize the ruthless wars by the assumption that they were supported by the universal God.

[350]Holtom also noted that discovery of traces of monotheistic universalism in the ancient foundations of Japanese national faith was originally made by [351]Atsutane Hirata (1776-1843) from Shinto scholarship, not from the Christian side. Hirata was a leader of the Restoration Shinto known as *Fukko Shinto* School. He was an outstanding scholar of his day who had drawn up an account of *Ame-no-Minakanushi-no-Kami* into which he had written a spiritual

349   Wikipedia: Kotoamatsukami. Online at http://en.wikipedia.org/wiki/Kotoamatsukami
350   D.C. Holtom. Modern Japan and Shinto Nationalism. (New York: USA Paragon Book Reprint Corp, 1963) pp. 115-116
351   Encyclopædia Britannica: Hirata Atsutane. Online at: http://www.britannica.com/eb/article-9040556/Hirata-Atsutane

monotheism that suggested the influence of the Christian idea of God. According to Holtom:

> Some of the later interpretations of Hirata have insisted that this is just what happened; that he studied and used discussions of Christian theology written by Jesuit missionaries in China and that for him to take over whatever he needed from this source and graft it onto a Shinto stem was entirely consistent with his conviction that by judicious selection from foreign writers Shinto should be made to include all the knowledge necessary to man (Holtom, 1963).

Hirata's discovery of the idea of an absolute and supreme God at the very beginning of the oldest Japanese document indicated that Shinto scholars during the Meiji era formulated the monotheistic interpretation of their foundational story written in Kojiki, perhaps under Christian influence. The main reason for the formulation of Shinto Monotheism was to justify Japan's military aggressions and to invade the territory of their neighbours by asserting that their action was condoned by the universal God, and also that the Japanese were the chosen race descended from Amaterasu, one of his offspring. Regarding Shinto-Christian collaboration to create Shinto monotheism, [352] Holtom states:

> It is undoubtedly true that those who support this doctrinal *reapproachment* between Christianity and Shinto are consciously and unconsciously led by the urgencies of stress and strain in political and social situation to seek an accommodation with Shinto which, while ostensibly bringing to fulfilment the latent truth of the national religion, will at the same time furnish Christianity with a protective apologetic much needed in time when it is under suspicion in certain influential

---

[352]   D.C. Holtom. Modern Japan and Shinto Nationalism. (New York, USA: Paragon Book Reprint Corp, 1963) p. 111

quarters as subversive of traditional institutions and belief (Holtom, 1963).

Christians, on the other hand, need citizenship in Japanese society and protection from the state to be engaged in their daily religious activities. Since Christianity was brutally persecuted during the era of Tokugawa Shogunate, they had a longing to be accepted by the public and to build a better relationship with the Meiji government. It seemed that Shinto and Christianity worked side by side for mutual benefits. [353]Although it was fully legitimate to follow the Pauline instruction to submit to the governing authority, some church leaders seemed to overemphasize the statement in the 13th chapter of Romans during the Meiji era. They crossed the accepted line of faith and seemed to teach, "Thou shall obey the government no matter how they act and treat their subjects." In order to obtain full citizenship in the Japanese society and to obtain the approval from the establishment, some Christians were seen to act in treason against Christ to the extent that in action they asserted the Godhead had four persons: The Father, the Son, the Holy Spirit, and Japanese Emperor. [354]It was blasphemy and similar to the action to yield their religious identity to the powerful force of Assyria and lose the entire dignity by eating their own excrement and drinking their own urine as well.

It was extremely unfortunate that Japanese Christians collaborated with Shinto nationalists to formulate rationale of the nation's imperialism and military aggressions all over East Asia. But Christian apologetics could use the discovery of some monotheistic aspects of the creation story in Kojiki to defend

353   Romans 13:1-5
354   Isaiah 36:11

the argument that monotheism existed before polytheism. In the beginning of all human history, every human individual believed in only one God and the polytheism was a product of the fall and a corruption of the original monotheism.

Ayako Sono (b.1931), a well-known Catholic writer, made the contemporary example of an attempt to compromise Christian faith and Japan's nationalism. She amalgamated Christian concepts and Shinto based Japanese nationalism, although she did not develop a systematic theology that embraced the divinity of the emperor like Akira Ebisawa. She visited Yasukuni annually and publicly declared that the visit was not contradictory with her Christian faith in any way.

[355]The amalgamation of Christianity and any other faith is not acceptable because it is against the first commandment to Moses. The underlined message behind the statement clearly communicated to us that God was the one who created us and was powerful enough to give us all the support we need. He is the only God we ever need.

Since Christianity has characteristics of a universal religion, it is not compatible with any form of nationalism. The entire theme of the Bible deals with only one God and all humans. The only distinction between people groups that the Bible recognizes is between those who belong to God and those who don't. Therefore the syncretism of Christianity with either a pagan belief system or any form of nationalism is considered apostasy and treason against God.

---

355   Exodus 20:1-3

Attempts to Proselytize Emperor Hirohito to Christianity

After Japan's defeat in the the Second World War and surrender, Gen. MacArthur made a decision to retain the monarchy, while he dismantled Shinto based Kokutai and reduced the emperor's role to a mere symbol. MacArthur tried hard to save the emperor from criminal prosecution and potential death penalty. When Japan's post Second World War government started under Prime Minister Yoshida, Hirohito denounced his divinity and declared that he was fully human.

He was also given opportunities to accept Jesus Christ. Some said he was once almost as convinced as [356]Herod Agrippa II who told Apostle Paul, "You almost persuade me to become a Christian." When he had a meeting with [357]Takeshi Saito (1887 – 1982), a well-known Christian academic, he listened earnestly as Saito explained Christian theology to the Emperor. Saito was one of many who seriously prayed for the conversion of Hirohito and tried to convince him that Jesus Christ was the one and only saviour in order that he might receive salvation. However, these attempts were futile and his conversion did not happen. Evil Kami of the nationalist cults including the Tennorei or the Imperial Spirit were not transferred into [358]swine from Hirohito's body. In the Bible, we find an account where Jesus drove out evil spirits from a man and transferred them into swine. Jesus as Lord, had authority over evil and as such he had the power to deliver the man from evil spirits.

---

356   Acts 26:28
357   Wikipedia: 斎藤勇 (イギリス文学者). Online at http://ja.wikipedia.org/wiki/%E6%96%8E%E8%97%A4%E5%8B%87_(%E3%82%A4%E3%82%AE%E3%83%AA%E3%82%B9%E6%96%87%E5%AD%A6%E8%80%85)
358   Matthew 8:32; Mark 5:13; Luke 8:33

Some Japanese Christians including Yuri Isshiki (died in 1953), Michi Kawai (1877-1953) and [359]Dr. Toyohiko Kagawa (1888–1960) attempted to rescue Hirohito and the emperor system by persuading General Headquarters (GHQ) officials of the Occupation Force including Gen. MacArthur to believe in Hirohito's innocence, possibly with the hope of winning his conversion later. Isshiki and Kawai who went to college with General Bonner Fellers, MacArthur's "military secretary," said that no grounds existed for holding the emperor responsible for the Pearl Harbor attack. Herbert Bix (2000) notes:

> [360]An entirely new, binational stage in the movement to protect Hirohito now began. Out of the interplay of efforts by GHQ, the emperor, Japanese government leaders, and Japanese Christians with prewar ties to influence Americans, came the shielding of Hirohito from war responsibility, his "humanization," and the reform of the imperial house (Bix, 2000).

[361]There was a time that both indigenous Japanese Christians and missionaries from overseas seriously attempted to disseminate Christian ethical, cultural and political ideals throughout all levels of Japanese society and even to proselytize Emperor Hirohito and his family. These Christians were probably thinking that Hirohito would come to Christ following a true repentance for everything he had done by giving him clemency and showing him extraordinary grace. But Hirohito simply took advantage of the charitable heart and good will of Christians. Some critics like [362]Hideaki Onizuka

---

359   Wikipedia: Toyohiko Kagawa. Online at http://en.wikipedia.org/wiki/Toyohiko_ Kagawa

360   Herbert P. Bix Hirohito and the Making of Modern Japan (NY: HarperCollins Publishers, 2000). P. 543

361   Ray Moor. Tenno ga Bible o yonda toki [Time when emperor read the Bible]. (Tokyo: Kodansha, 1982)

362   Hideaki Onizuka. Tenno no Rosario [Rosario of the emperor]. (Tokyo: Junkudo, 1995)

(1995) note that Hirohito sometimes showed a pose to be interested in the Christianity and flashed around the possibility of conversion simply to give a good impression to Gen. MacArthur and leaders in Washington.

I personally believe that these Christians should not have helped the emperor unless he demonstrated genuine remorse for what he had done, accepting responsibility for the war and readiness to accept Christian faith following the abandonment of the Shinto belief system. What Hirohito did after the war was somehow similar to criminals or *jailbirds* who attend Bible studies and sometimes have dramatic "born-again" experiences only when they are in prison. Some of these prisoners have the same "born-again" experiences several times whenever they commit crimes and later go back in prison. Unfortunately, the Christian individuals with good will and charitable hearts assisted the survival of not merely Hirohito as a person but also the emperor system, leaving the potential of resurrection of the demonic Kokutai prior to the Second World War. Ironically, it was believed that Shigeru Yoshida, an adamant loyalist who forced the emperor to remain in the Shinto tradition, accepted Jesus Christ through his Roman Catholic wife and daughter shortly before his death in 1967 like [363]a thief who was crucified with Lord Jesus.

It was speculated among some Japanese that Hirohito had expressed his wish to abdicate or retire from the throne from time to time. Nevertheless, he remained in the Throne of Chrysanthemum until his death at 89. Hirohito's persistence to remain on the throne resembled a man living in a grave possessed by [364]*Legion,* a multitude of demons in the New

363   Luke 23:42-43
364   Matthew 8:28-34; Mark 5:1-20; Luke 8:28-33

Testament. In the same way, *Kami* that belonged to the State Shinto or imperial cult did not release him from the throne. According to the Bible, Jesus travelled to "the country of the Gadarenes" and met a man possessed by an evil spirit, which spoke to Jesus in a conversation. In Mark 5:9, when Jesus asked his name, the man responded by saying, "My name is Legion: for we are many" (KJV). In fact, Shinto has thousands of Kami or deities whom they revere and worship. State Shinto and Kokutai or the spiritual community centred on the emperor, were the condominium in which unclean spirits resided. Of course, in a tomb there were no real lives of human beings. Only ghosts, eerie spiritual beings, demons, half-demons or vampires would like to live there. Hirohito's very role as the high priest of the State Shinto and centre of Kokutai was a custodian of the condominium for the demons and unclean spirits. As Bix notes, Hirohito had an appearance of trying to maintain the throne and emperor system by all means with the cost of all soldiers and civilians' life. In my understanding, it explained that he was a custodian of the graveyard who was bound by these spirits.

This is reminiscent of [365]In *Spirited Away* (2001), one of Hayao Miyazaki's famous animation films, a young girl named *Chihiro Ogino* finds herself slipping into a mysterious and eerie spiritual world. She is moving to a new town with her parents and is clearly unhappy about the move and appears rather petulant. The family loses its way and comes across a tunnel, which they enter out of curiosity, unaware that it actually provides access into a spirit world—specifically, to a spirit bathhouse, in which spirits of the Shinto religion go to

---

365   Wikipedia: Spirited Away. Online at http://en.wikipedia.org/wiki/Spirited_Away

rest and relax. She meets a witch named Yubaba who looks like an elderly woman and owns a bathhouse. Chihiro ends up working for the bathhouse there serving various kinds of *Kami* or spiritual beings. The customers whom she has to serve were Kami instead of humans. For Yubaba, an elderly and monstrous lady who owned the bathhouse, humans were despicable, worthless creatures whom she had nothing to do with.

Syncretism with Bushido

But even long time before the *Religious Organization Law* was enacted, Japanese Christianity was subject to the syncretism of some indigenous thoughts, since it was a small and weak minority. According to [366]D.C. Holtom (1963), Japanese Christianity made a couple of significant syncretistic moves during the Meiji era. One was quite a benign synchronization with [367]*Bushido* (武士道), meaning "Way of the Warrior or Samurai," which was typical code of ethics among "warrior class" people prior to the Meiji Restoration. Bushido developed between the 11th to 14th centuries as set forth by numerous translated documents dating from the 12th to 16th centuries. Holtom maintains there was a unique correspondence between Christianity and Bushido.

[368]Inazo Nitobe (1862 - 1933), a well known Christian Educator and author in the late Meiji era, wrote a book about *Bushido* targeted to Western readers. In his book [369]*Bushido:*

---

366   D.C. Holtom. Modern Japan and Shinto Nationalism. (New York: USA Paragon Book Reprint Corp, 1963) p. 39
367   Wikipedia: Bushidō. Online at http://en.wikipedia.org/wiki/Bushido
368   Wikipedia: Nitobe Inazō. Online at http://en.wikipedia.org/wiki/Nitobe_Inaz%C5%8D
369   Inazo Nitobe. Bushido: The Soul of Japan: An Exposition of Japanese Thought. (Tokyo: Japan Kodansha International, 1900/2002)

the Soul of Japan (1900), Nitobe described that Bushido was the code of moral principles that the Samurai were required or instructed to observe. It was a code and way of life for Samurai, a class of warriors similar to the medieval knights of Europe. Zen Buddhism and Confucianism, two different schools of thought of those periods, also influenced the code. More frequently it was an unuttered and unwritten code, and then it had an organic growth of decades and centuries of military career among "Samurai class." For Nitobe, the practice of Bushido or code of Samurai was equal to living a good Christian life.

Regarding the similarities between Bushido and Christianity, [370]Saburo Imai (1940), a former Methodist pastor in Japan, stated that Bushido was founded on a strong sense of moral obligation and held the doctrine of sacrificial death. The almost stoic moral obligation was easily identified with Christian ethics and the code of self-sacrifice had association with the sacrificial death of Christ and the highly disciplined life of the apostle Paul as a "libation" poured out to the glory of God[371].

In fact, [372]the majority of Christians from the Meiji era were from the Samurai class who sided on the Tokugawa Shogunate during the Boshin War, and therefore had an anti-Meiji Restorationist sentiment. This syncretism of Christianity and Bushido took place in the moral and ethical domain rather than spiritual domain. Therefore it was harmless and rather beneficial and the former Samurai class Christians had

---

370   Saburo Imai. Seishin Hokoku to Kirisuto Kyo [Patriotism of the Spirit and Christianity]. (Tokyo, 1940)
371   Philippians 2:17-18
372   Yasuo Furuya. A History of Japanese Theology. (Grand Rapid: Michigan. William B. Eerdmans Publishing Company, 1963) p. 39

an advantage that they could transfer their code of ethics into the new life as believers. These *Samurai Christians* lived the new life in Christ with a rather counter-cultural and anti-establishment sentiment against the Meiji government and the evil State Shinto.

Mitsuo Fuchida, God's Samurai

[373]Mitsuo Fuchida (1902 - 1976), the former Imperial naval career aviator who led the attack on Pearl Harbor and participated in most of the fiercest battles of the Pacific War, became a believer in Christ after the war and spent the rest of his life as an evangelist until his death in 1976. Regarding his background as a soldier, he said, "Because my father was a primary school principal and a very patriotic nationalist, I was able to enroll in the Naval Academy when I was 18. Upon graduation three years later, I joined the Japanese Naval Air Force, and served mostly as an aircraft carrier pilot for the next 15 years (Prange, 1963).

After the war, in 1949, Fuchida encountered a Free Methodist missionary named Jake DeShazer, himself a former U.S. Army Air Force Corporal and a pilot of a bomber who was shot down and captured as a prisoner in Japan. Shortly thereafter Fuchida converted to Christianity. He also identified himself as a [374]*God's Samurai* during his entire carrier as a minister. As an Imperial soldier, he followed the same Bushido tradition with a strong sense of moral obligation and self-sacrifice as those who lived 100 years prior. So after conversion he easily identified himself as a Samurai Christian as those who converted to Christ in the Meiji era. The Bushido

373   Wikipedia: Mitsuo Fuchida. Online at http://en.wikipedia.org/wiki/Mitsuo_Fuchida
374   Gordon W. Prange, Goldstein, Donald M., Dillon, Katherine V. God's Samurai: Lead Pilot at Pearl Harbor. (New York: USA Paragon Book Reprint Corp, 1963)

or the code of ethics among Samurai class people motivated Japanese Christians to endeavor for achievement parallel with the Apostle Paul's self-identification as a warrior of God who lived a disciplined life to be the [375]winner of the ultimate race and receive the prize.

[376]Tokyo Union Theological Seminary.

---

375   1 Corinthians 9:24
376   The picture is taken by the author, 2008.

6

Conclusion

During the past two millenia, the Japanese have developed the concept of the preternatural world including life after death and various physical and non-physical life forms living in different demensions of the universe. They have incorporated various ideas on the spiritual and supernatural realm of the universe as well as various pictures of the afterlife. This magnificent and grandiose preternatural worldview is also demonstrated in the Anime and Manga world as well as the contemporary Japanese literature.

The rudimental part of their preternatural worldview is the archaic shamanistic Shinto belief developed in the Jomen Period long time before the writing system was introduced to the archipelago from the continent. According this belief, all living beings continue to rotate in the cycle of life and death and take various forms somewhat randomly from the eternal past to the eternal future. The concept of morality was completely foreign to the Shinto based animistic world and the residents of Japan prior to the introduction of Buddhism and Confucianism from the continent. The primitive Shinto, however, believed in magic or shamanic spells to change the destiny of an individual or a whole nation.

The rulers of archaic Japan were magi or shaman kings and queens like the three Eastern Kings who visited Bethlehem when Christ was born, and practiced magics and sorceries as they governed the nation[377]. Therefore, the ancestors of the Japanese emperor were Shinto high priests, shamanic kings and queens with the belief in powers to change the fate and destiny of the whole nation. In primitive Shinto, religion was a tool to change people's destiny through spells and divinations instead of establishing the morality of the whole nation. Survival in a harsh natural environment was the first and utmost priority for the primitive island nation of antiquity. In the process of divinations, the priests slaughtered all kinds of animals just as any many other primitive religions on the planet, and dared to sacrifice even live humans. Although there are no written documents or any concrete evidences to prove it, there is a likelihood that the carnibalism and human sacrifice for the religious rites were practiced in order to promote the wellbeing of the community, just as many other pre-historic barbaric societies.

After the Asuka Period, philosophies like Buddhism, Taoism, Confucianism and a new state-governing system were introduced to the nation from the continent and Japan became a more civilized society. The synchronization of Shinto and Buddhism made the nation a society with the dual faith of two different belief systems and gave their afterlife concept more complexity and sophistication. After the introduction of the Buddhist teaching, Japanese also developed the custom of self-immolation or suicidal ritual which aimed at post-mortem transformation into Bodhisattva. People drew various

---

377   Matthew 2:1-26

magnificent pictures of good and bad afterlife and the Buddhist religion flourished during the Heian period. Imaginative writers also created stories about paranormal incidents such as activities of the ghosts of the deads who failed to transform into Bodhisattva and stay in this world without bodies as well as mischevous animal spirits in the medieval age folklore.

The modernity of the nation started in the mid-Muromachi Period, was characterized by the industrialization and Westernization. In a technological sense, Japan made a significant transition from the Middle Age to the modernity during this period, following the example of powerful Western nations. However, they had little changes in the socio-political and psycho-spiritual domain of the nation until the Meiji Restoration that took place in 1868.

Christianity migrated into the archipelago in the mid-Muromachi Period along with new technology from the West. The new faith was quickly dispersed into the whole nation and was once about to permeate through the Samurai class citizens there. Christianity gave a completely new hope to the citizens who were tired of the endless conflicts among greedy and worldly Buddhist monks. However, the light of the newly developed faith among the island nation was extinguished by a series persecutions by both Toyotomi and early Tokugawa's regimes. In 1637 during the reign of Tokugawa Iemitsu, nearly all Japanese Christians were annihilated after an armed revolt led by a Samurai class Christian called Amakusa Shirō Tokisada in a small community named Shimabara in Kyushu. Since then, Christianity was totally banned and outlawed, and all believers were executed unless they recanted their faith. Since then, the nation was completely segregated from the influence of Christianity. Neverthless, non-Christian spiritualities like Western paganism, witchcraft and occultism like the *Ouija board* from the West and easily immigrated to Japan through the sailors from the Netherlands and continued to influence the island nation during the era of the total seclusion.

After the Meiji Restoration in 1868, the ban against Christianity was lifted, and many former Samurai class warriors converted to Christianity. Once converted, they became dedicated, serious and passionate believers. In the Meiji Period, Protestant denominations also entered for the first time and started vigorous missionary work. However, newly revived Christianity in Japan had to face new enemies seemingly more evil and demonic than the Tokugawa shogunate. They are *State Shinto* and a totalitarian regeme in which the emperor was the sacred and inviolable head of the state. Under *Meiji Constitution* and *Imperial Rescript on Education*, Christians were forced to agree with the constitution and the educational rescript that stipulated the divinity of the emperor that contradicted with Christian principles. Many were persecuted by the new regime for denying the divinity of the emperor, while some compromised their theology and embraced the teaching of the State Shinto. Also, under the Religious Organization Law enacted shortly before the Second World War, all religious organizations including Christian churches had to comply with strict government policy to apply for and be granted government recognition to operate legally. The recognition depended on the religious body's agreement to teach rites supportive of the emperor's divinity and other Shinto based worldviews. Persecutions continued until the total defeat of the Imperial Japan in the Second World War in 1945.

After the war, Japanese Christians obtained complete liberty to worship the one and only God instead of the emperor and many false gods. However, the task of evangelism struggled for decades, and Christian population there has remained less than one percent of the total population under democracy in the 2010s. The largest reason that Japanese Christianity suffers in a most peaceful and liberated era may owe to their Shinto based cultural soil, in which the concept of sin and transgression is completely foreign. In Neon Genesis Evangelion (1995)[378], an anime movie created by Hideaki Anno (b.1960)[379], a female army officer made an interesting statement, "Bath is a laundry of life" in the second episode. This indicates the Shinto based philosophy of the author, because a cleansing ritual with water is an extremely important part of Shintoism. The motif of Shinto deities having baths could also be observed in Hayao Miyazaki's Spirited Away (2001)[380]. Various Shinto Kami gather in Yubaba's bathhouse where Chihiro works in order to clean themselves or do the "laundry of life"[381]. According to the Shinto philosophy, the laundry of life is good enough to remove the stain and defilement of the humanity and therefore the redeeming blood of the Saviour is a completely foreign and redundant concept.

State Shinto was a spirituality created in the modern era that led the entire nation into a series of wars and a

---

378   Wikipedia: Neon Genesis Evangelion. Online at http://en.wikipedia.org/wiki/Neon_Genesis_Evangelion
379   Wikipedia: Hideaki Anno. Online at http://en.wikipedia.org/wiki/Hideaki_Anno
380   Wikipedia: Spirited Away. Online at http://en.wikipedia.org/wiki/Spirited_Away
381   Isao Ebihara. All the World IS Anime. (Dayton, TN: USA: Global Ed Advance, 2010)

total destruction at the end. State Shinto, which was closely associated with the emperor system and militarism, had a clear distinction from the original Shinto. According to this belief system, the emperor was a living god who was a descendant of the great Sun Goddess *Amaterasu*. All imperial soldiers were taught that dying for the emperor was a glorified act pertaining to the greatest honor for the Japanese.

During the Meiji Period, several new religions including Oomoto-kyo came into existence. Onisaburō Deguchi became the head of the organization to establish a new doctrine in which traditional Shinto and Buddhist beliefs are integrated with Western philosophies and spiritualities like Scientism. There was also a time that the organization was named Kōdō Ōmoto (皇道大本) or "Omoto Imperial Way" and was forced to follow the government policy to embrace State Shinto and the emperor's divinity like all other religious organizations.

Many anime and manga authors after the Second World War created fantastic stories about the preternatural domain of the universe following the theme of traditional ghost stories and folklore and typical Japanese spiritual tradition. Anime and manga based on the worldwide Otaku culture is a powerful impetus to demolish traditional national and ethnic boundries and create one unified larger global community. The era of globalism has drastically changed the Western world as well as Asia and the rest of the world. In the 21st century, the Western nations are not simply West and Asia is not simply Asia in the same way as previous centuries. Likewise, Japan is not Japan in the traditional sense and she will soon lose her national identity just as all other sovereign nation-states on this planet. There will be a glimpse of hope for Christian evangelism when

the impacts of globalization utterly demolish the national
boundries and finally liberate residents of the archipelago from
the traditional "Japaneseness" and Shinto way of thinking.

[382] Shigeru Mizuki's Konaki Jijii [383].

382   Shigeru Mizuki. Shigeru Mizuki's Yōkai Map. Hebonsha, Tokyo: Japan, 2011.
383   The picture is used under "fair dealing" (Canada) and "fair use" (USA) provisions
in copyright law.

Glossary

Bodhisattva A small Buddha, an enlightened (bodhi) existence (sattva) or an enlightenment-being

Dharmadhatu The 'dimension' or 'realm' of Dharma which means Natural Law and a concept of central importance in Indian philosophy and religion. It designates behaviours necessary for the maintenance of the natural order of things.

Kami (神) A god, deity or spirit in Shinto mythology. The Japanese term "Kami" also refers to monotheistic God in Judeo Christian tradition.

Kannon (観音) Japanese name of the Guanyin, a bodhisattva or goddess associated with compassion and mercy

Miroku (弥勒) Japanese name of the Buddha Maitreya or the great future Buddha.

Satori (悟り) A Japanese Buddhist term for enlightenment, with the literal meaning "understanding"

About the Author

Isao Ebihara, D.Phil. (Oxford Graduate School, TN), a native of Japan, has resided in Canada for over 20 years. He has taught Japanese language courses at Trinity Western University in British Colombia since 2002. His academic training encompasses theology, psychology and literature, and his interests include Japanese language, Asian animation and pop culture, culture and spirituality and religions and politics.

Dr. Ebihara has a thorough knowledge of Japanese anime culture and recognizes its great impact on the global community. In his 2010 book, *All the World is Anime: Religions, Myths & Spiritual Metaphors in the World of Japanimation & Manga*, he explored the philosophical and religious/spiritual background of the anime authors and stories and a history of their productions.

In his 2011 book, *Shinto War Gods of Yasukuni Shrine: The Gates of Hades and Japan's Emperor Cult*, Dr. Ebihara made a comparison of the cultural and historical components of Shinto religion to pop cultures including anime (Japanese animations) and manga (Japanese comics), drawing upon the work of Alan J.P. Taylor's populist or "anti-great man" approach and Carl Jung's archetype theory.

In this book, Dr. Ebihara examines the world of ghosts, spirits, supernatural phenomena and incidents in Japanese mythology, folklore and legends from antiquity to novels and today's modern tales of anime and manga.